BRAZIL

PLACES AND HISTORY

STEWART, TABORI & CHANG
NEW YORK

CONTENTS

Text
Beppe Ceccato

Art Director
Patrizia Balocco

Editing Supervision by
Valeria Manferto De Fabianis
Laura Accomazzo

Graphic Supervision by
Anna Galliani

Translation by
Barbara Fisher
A.B.A.

1 *The statue of Christ the Redeemer was inaugurated in 1931. It is the work of the French sculptor Paul Landowsky and stands 100 feet high on Corcovado, in Rio de Janeiro.*

2–7 *This elaborate map shows Brazil in 1642, when the Dutch wanted to expand their control of the country's northeast coast.*

3–6 *Pão de Açúcar is a granite peak at the entrance to the Guanábara Bay. There is an unusual story about its name: The Indians called it Pau-nd-Acuqua, solitary peak, but to*

the ears of the Portuguese it sounded like Pão de Açúcar, sugarloaf, and its distinctive cone shape resembled the clay molds they used to make sugar loaves.

Acknowledgment

To Sonia, who helped me to see, understand, and love this remarkable country.

Copyright © White Star S.r.l.
Via Sassone, 22/24
13100 Vercelli, Italy

Published in 1998 and distributed in the U.S. by
Stewart, Tabori & Chang,
a division of U.S. Media Holdings, Inc.
115 West 18th Street, New York, NY 10011

Distributed in Canada by
General Publishing Ltd.
30 Lesmill Road, Don Mills
Ontario, M3B 2T6, Canada

Library of Congress Catalog Card Number:
97-68225

ISBN 1-55670-691-X

Printed in Italy

10 9 8 7 6 5 4 3 2 1

First Edition

Epuremei

Arowaccas pop

R. negro

Davume lago

Muchikeri

C. Droge C.N
Macureuwaray

E.Huys vande
G.van peere

Parinaquacu

Tilnada

Chirmos

Tabo

R. delas Amazones

Harrytiahans

Caribes Iaios
Aravaca

puerto de
los Reyes

R. de los Topajos

Bocas de Para
grade Para

C. d'Orange
C.Cassepoure

C. Noord

Aldea de Irorapian
Rante de Mel
Rengere Riu
Marapo
R. Naua
R. Itata
R. Surina
Surianamo
Paraquatos
R. Flaman

R. Loraque: R. S. Paule

Raris

R. Maradi

MARAGNAN.

I. Maranhon

BRASIL

SPLRITV

R. Pereya
R. Laerhug
R. Maripa

R. de Pergue
R. Camindei
Otottpy

Paraguashi O R. de Para

R. Iguarasu

R. Iosara
Guapanins

R. de Camucige O R. S. Francisca
Nua Sro de rosario

Sababuba
Oreatdunerin

CAPITANIA DE
PORTO SEGVRO
Aymures
Guaynuves
Cap. DE LOS
Illeos

Cap. d. Sirra
o. Ciara

Tortugas P.

Araxetos R. d Cruz
R. Pernambuco
R. Alman R. Mondubug
Turiuhu
R. Tacara R. Cojubu
R. Cornil
R. Seubha
Pta. de Arecifes
Pta de Cabo des Siam
R. de Iguape
Lapanaso
R. Lagzariti

Itarihon

Cap. DE BAHIA DE
TODO SANCTOS

PVYA

R. Vijustiguarra
Pta. de Mel
R. Camaraba
R. Guapohina
Roobco
Soulp in Caranamet
R. Comara
Pto. Cassi

Topi
manbaxes
Quites
Mata

Cap. DE PERNAMBVC
Cap. DE TAMARACA
Cap. DE R. GRANDE

Baxos de St. Roque

Tamaraca

Roca

Duytsche mylen 15 op een graedt.
10   20   30   40   50   60
Spaensche leguas 17½ op een graedt
10   20   30   40   50   60   70
Engelsche en 'Fransche mylen 20 op een graedt
10   20   30   40   50   60   70   80

Vigu

LINEA AEQVINOCTIALIS

*A*na Maria da Conceição, 57, comes from Colônia de Leopoldina, a small town in Alagoas State, in the north of Brazil. She's been living in São Paulo for 30 years, having journeyed to the city like thousands of other northeasterners in search of a job and a better life. Ana didn't find a job, just occasional work as a *faxineira* (charwoman). She didn't even find a better life; she's been living for 10 years in a sewer pipe with a

diameter of 4 feet on Marginal Pinheiros, the orbital motorway that is one of the most polluted parts of São Paulo. Every time it rains, she has to run out into the street to avoid being swept away by the force of the water.

Two hundred seventeen miles farther west, in the town of Bauru, also in São Paulo State, Dr. Gastão, a friendly gentlemen who collects statuettes of St. Francis, runs the Centro de Riabilitação das Lesões Labio Palatais (Labiopalatine Malformation Rehabilitation Center), nicknamed the "Centrinho" ("little center") by the residents of the city. The Centrinho specializes in repairing malformations such as harelip and cleft palate and is the leading hospital of its kind in South America. It conducts advanced studies, and doctors come from as far away as the United States to learn about new developments in the subject. The hospital is open to all, rich and poor alike, and treatment is free.

These are just two of the hundreds of everyday stories typical of the largest country in South America. Total indigence and sophisticated technology, a high illiteracy rate and top-level universities, avant-garde architecture and cardboard shantytowns—this mass of contradictions is Brazil in the 1990s.

After 13 years of military dictatorship, the country plunged into an unprecedented recession, fell into the clutches of unscrupulous presidents, and was put back on its feet by an

10–11 *Dancing is a moment of aggregation in the* aldeias, *the native villages. Men and women never dance together. Only in the upper Xingu do the women dance resting their hand on the shoulder of their partner.*

10 top left
Indian tribal chiefs are distinguished by their refined feather headdresses and large wooden inserts in their lips. The chiefs, or cacique, *are chosen according to the customs of the different tribes. Among the Borór Indians, for instance, leadership does not pass from father to son but through maternal descent. The life led by the cacique is similar to that of the other members of the tribe, and leaders have no special privileges.*

10 top right
A small Kayapó Indian wearing a traditional costume. Her face is painted with a vegetable dye called urucu, *which is obtained from the seeds of the arnotto* (Bixa orellana), *a tree characteristic of tropical America with leaves similar to those of the lime tree.*

economic plan that has reduced inflation and stabilized the currency but not increased the amount of money in people's pockets. Despite these difficulties, Brazil is still perceived as the land of fun, the Carnival of Rio, football, and pretty mulatto girls who offer their sensual curves at cut price. It's true that sensuality and joie de vivre *are* typical of the Brazilians. But the country is also full of contrasts, from the civilized south, home of Curitiba, the model town where bus stops are designed so people with handicaps can get on and off buses easily and there's no litter in the streets, not even a cigarette butts; to the lively chaos of Salvador in the northeast, the first city founded by the Portuguese, the center of Afro-Brazilian culture, and the realm of Candomblé and the Yoruba deities; and cities like the huge São Paulo and the classic Rio de Janeiro, with its gently smiling statue of Christ the Redeemer, arms permanently outstretched to bless Guanábara Bay. These very different cities are in a country that is larger than Western Europe and shares the same principles in life.

Brazil's people have a mild, gentle, humorous character and are always ready to joke. Their origin no longer matters: Italians and Arabs, Japanese and Africans have merged to become Brazilians. "I get annoyed when people say I should cultivate my African roots," says Carlinhos Brown, a well-known musician from Bahia. "I'm

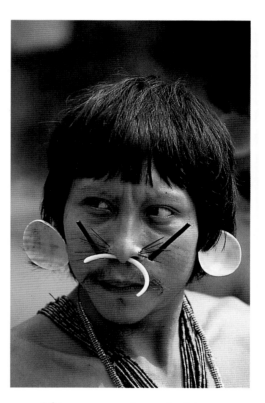

not African; my culture is this one, a combination of several cultures. I'm a Brazilian." It's no accident that, apart from sporadic episodes, Brazil has not produced revolutionary movements like the Shining Path in Peru, the Montoneros in Argentina, and the Sandinistas in Nicaragua. Brazilians are known for being tolerant. It does not make headlines when street children are brutally murdered by death squads; it's not even news that, despite the interest of singers, politicians, and scientists, Amazonia is inexorably heading toward destruction. None of these events seem to matter because they're just a routine part of everyday life—normal occurrences in a Third World country. Even the country's economic recession, terrible poverty,

12–13 *São João del Rei is a well-preserved colonial town in Minas Gerais. It is famous for the splendid church of São*

Francisco de Assís, surrounded by towering coqueros imperiais, coconut palms more than 130 feet high, and as the

birthplace of Tancredo Neves, one of the best-loved Brazilian politicians who died in mysterious circumstances.

and social injustice are no longer newsworthy to Brazilians. So the country's next anniversary, in the year 2000, may pass unnoticed.

After five centuries, Brazil is still young and brimming with natural resources, imagination, and adaptability. The challenge facing its government is to give 180 million people the opportunity to go to school, get a job, and believe in a slightly fairer Brazil. Impossible? Perhaps. But with Brazilians, you never can tell.

13 top
The Amazonas Theater opera house in Manaus was built in 1896 during the height of the rubber boom that brought riches to the city. At the time, Manaus was one of the most important river ports in the world.

13 bottom
The Church of São Francisco de Assis, in Salvador, dates from the 18th century and was built with stones brought from Portugal. The interior, a triumph of colonial baroque style, is filled with gold-leaf-covered inlays. More than 100 pounds of this precious metal was used to decorate the church.

Venezuela

Colombia

Guyana

Suriname

French Guyana

Pernambuco coast

Marajó Island

Manaus

Santarém

Belém

São Luís

Fortaleza

Amazon River

Recife

Palmares

Xingu River

Araguaia River

Tocantins River

São Francisco River

Serra do Roncador

Salvador

Peru

Mato Grosso

Cuiabá

Brasília

Goiânia

Todos os Santos Bay

Porto Seguro

Bolivia

The Pantanal

Paraguay

Paraná River

Belo Horizonte

Ouro Prêto

Aracruz

Paraguay River

Bauru

Rio de Janeiro

Chile

São Paulo

Curitiba

Argentina

Patos Lagoon

Mirim Lagoon

Uruguay

Atlantic Ocean

The valley of Bocaina, in Saõ Paulo

16–17 *The Matriz de São Antônio in Tiradentes is an exultation of stucco and gold. It is said to be second only to São Francisco de Assís in Salvador for the quantity of gold (more than half a ton) used. Tiradentes is a pretty colonial town that takes its name from a dentist (or tiradentes), Joaquim José da Silva Xavier, who was head of the Inconfidência independence movement of 1789. Betrayed, he was captured and butchered by the Portuguese.*

18–19 *The rivers of the Amazon can be divided into three types: with white, brown, or transparent waters. The first, like the Amazon River itself, are rich in sediments that make the water usually whitish-yellow; the second have acid water lacking in mineral nutrients; and the third have a reduced suspension content.*

Fernando de Noronha Archipelago

Amazon River near Santarém

A stretch of fluvial plants in Pantanal

O n April 21, 1500, young Pedro Álvars Cabral, commanding 13 ships that had set sail from the Tagus River in Lisbon on March 8 the same year, cried out for joy. After leaving behind the Cape Verde Islands, which were ruled by the Lusitanian crown, he had sailed west and finally sighted land. According to his calculations, he had discovered a new route to the Indies. In fact, the navigator had sighted the beaches of Porto Seguro in what is now the State of Bahia, Brazil.

Christopher Columbus made the same mistake eight years earlier, when, acting on behalf of the powerful Spanish crown, he landed on American soil (in the West Indies), convinced that he had sailed the China Sea and reached India.

20 Pedro Álvars Cabral claims the newly discovered land for the Portuguese crown, for King Manuel I. Some historians believe that the Brazilian coasts were visited by the Portuguese before 1500, the official year of discovery.

20–21 Cabral landed in Brazil, on the coast of what is now Porto Seguro on April 22, 1500. The day before, April 21, the Portuguese admiral and his fleet disembarked near Porto Seguro. The painting, kept in the National History Museum in Rio de Janeiro, is by Oscár Pereira da Silva (1867–1939).

The 13 ships with which Pedro Álvars Cabral sailed from Lisbon's Tagus River on March 9, 1500, are shown here in a 1565 reproduction from Lisuarte de Abreu's book, which is kept in New York's Pierpont Morgan Library.

22–23 The 1494 Treaty of Tordesillas (Tordesilhas in Portuguese), shown here in a painting by Antonio Menendez and conserved in the Naval Museum in Lisbon, fixed new boundaries between the Spanish and Portuguese colonial empires (approximately 370 miles west of Cape Verde) in favor of Portugal.

22 top John II (1455–1495), king of Portugal, encouraged Portuguese expansionism. During his reign the Azores, Madeira, Cape Verde, and São Tomé were discovered and claimed, assuring ivory trade, slaves, and gold for his country. Portugal acted as an intermediary, purchasing gold and slaves from Guinea and exchanging them for products from Flanders, Germany, Italy, England, and France, which were then sold through Flanders on the European market.

23 top
*The Treaty of
Tordesillas modified
Pope Alexander VI's
(1431-1503) Inter
Caetera bull of 1493,
which divided the
world up in favor of
the Spanish crown.*

The result of Columbus's discoveries
was the Treaty of Tordesillas, signed
on June 7, 1494, by John II of Portugal and Ferdinand and Isabella of
Spain. The treaty modified the division of the world, pronounced the
previous year by Pope Alexander VI in
the Papal Bull *Inter Caetera*, in favor
of Portugal. The Portuguese crown,
assisted by Duarte Pacheco Pereira, a
specialist in geography and cosmogra-
phy who attended the conference (and
was also one of the captains of
Cabral's ships), was authorized to take
possession of all lands (and all inhabitants) of the New World that lay 370
leagues west of Cape Verde.

23 bottom
An excelente, *a
16th-century Spanish
gold coin. The coin's
faces depict
Ferdinand of Aragon
and Isabella of
Castile. Christopher
Columbus
"discovered" America
in 1492 during their
reign.*

24–25 *In the native communities, the men hunted and defended the tribe, and women devoted themselves to agriculture and craftwork. Europeans initially found the Indians to be exotic, and they exhibited them in the European courts, as in this representation of native life in Rouen, France, in 1550.*

24 top left
In the chronicles of the times, provided by Jesuits and colonists, "good Indians" allied with the Portuguese; all the others who fought against them were bad. The Aimoré, *for instance, who differed from the other tribes in their military efficiency and rebel spirit, were always described by the chroniclers as animals living in the forest. When the first law banning Indian slavery was published in 1570 only the Aimoré were specifically excluded.*

24 top right
During colonization the Indians barely survived, procuring only the essentials for the consumption of the tribe. They felled trees and burned the forest to cultivate wheat, beans, marrows, and manioc, a root that became a staple in Brazil. There were contacts between tribes who exchanged women and luxury goods, toucan feathers, and the stones to make botoques (ornamental objects).

25 top
Convinced he had discovered the Indies, Cabral baptized these Amerindian peoples "Indians." It is hard to analyze the society and customs of the Indians because their entire history has been filtered by the Portuguese, who considered certain beliefs and habits to be barbarous.

Young Cabral, convinced that he had dropped anchor in the Indian Ocean, named the strange people who watched the large ships that had appeared out of nowhere "Indians." At that time, the population of Brazil was mainly concentrated in the coastal area of the country and the Paraná–Paraguay river basin to the south.

Brazil's native population was unrelated to the native peoples encountered by the Spanish in Central America and on the east coast of South America; the Mayas were skilled observers of the stars, the Incas sophisticated jewelers and weavers, and the Aztecs had built an empire that impressed the conquistadors. The native Brazilians (divided into two main races, Tupi-Guarani and Tapuiá) still lived in a semiprimitive state. They were sociable and simple; the women made pottery and farmed the land, planting beans, corn, pumpkins, and above all cassava (cassava flour later became a staple in the colony), while the men hunted, fished, and defended the villages.

The arrival of the Portuguese was a catastrophe for the Indians. The discovery of Brazil can undoubtedly be described as one of the worst holocausts in history. The Indians were enslaved, exterminated by diseases unknown to them, and forced to lead a life of hard toil and to give up their ancient customs. The church contributed to the tyranny with directives and local interventions that supported the colonial policy of the two European superpowers; "the souls are God's and the land is the king's" was the Pope's motto.

25 bottom
The Indians who lived in Brazil when the Portuguese landed were Tupi-Guaranis. The encounter with European culture for these peoples, who were not a nation proper but different tribes often at odds with each other, was devastating.

26 top left, right, center, and bottom right, and 27 top right
The Botocudos Indians pierced their earlobes, nose, and chin to insert botoques *(stone disks). The piercings occurred during childhood. The mouth inserts, now used by the Cayapó, deform the dental arch, curving it inward.*

26 top right
The Tupi-Guarani Indians were nomads and frequently changed village according to the food and crops they managed to produce. With the arrival of the Portuguese, the natives withdrew into ever less explored and hospitable areas for protection.

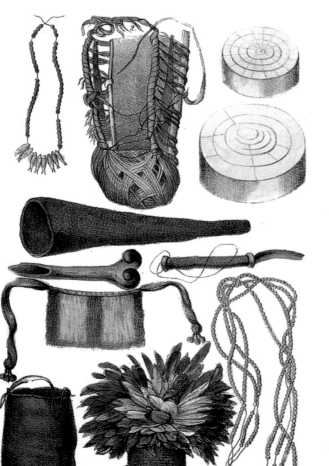

26 bottom left
The objects used by the Brazilian Indians (seen here in a 1841 lithograph from the Galleria Universale di Tutti i Populi del Mondo, Venice, were simple but decorative.

26–27 The Indians had a strong sense of family. The members of the same tribe usually lived in aldeias (large huts) and shared everything.

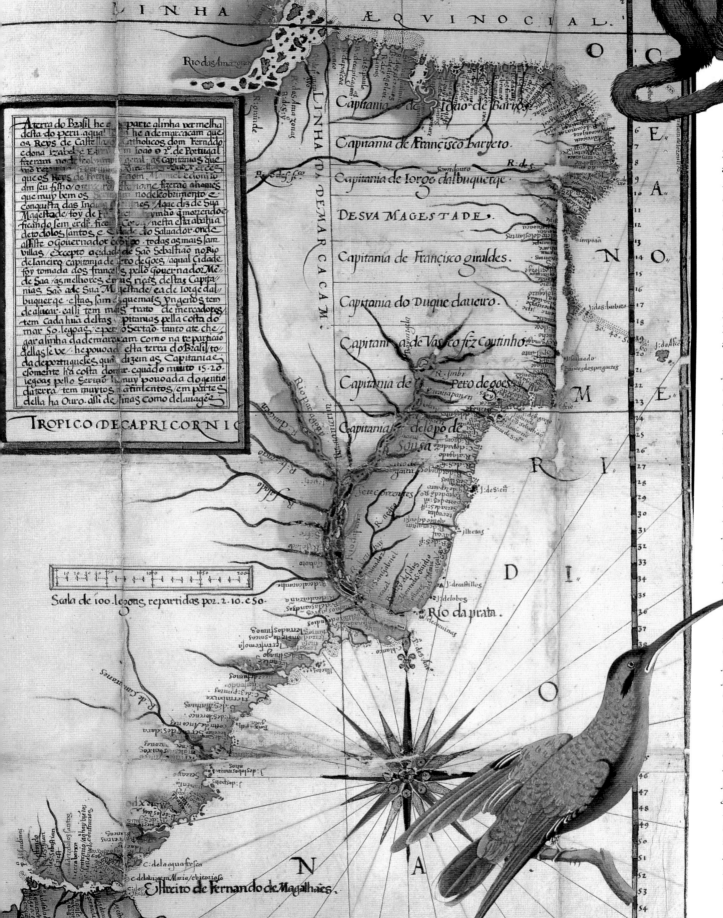

28 left

The coast of Brazil in 1579, 80 years after its discovery, in a print of the period kept in the Ajuda Library in Lisbon.

28 top right and 29 top
Monkeys, like tropical birds, struck the imagination of the colonists and were imported to many courts in Europe, to the gain of the traders.

28 bottom right, 29 center right, and 29 bottom
Tropical birds fascinated the colonists, who started a flourishing trade to Europe. They traded araras, large parrots, toucans, and numerous species of hummingbirds.

29 center left
A nautical chart from 1540 shows the Brazilian coasts. After an initial period of adjustment, trade with Portugal intensified. The mercantilist policy of Portugal gave a sort of monopoly to boats flying the national flag: They were the only ones allowed to carry the products of the colony to Portugal. This was done in an attempt to stop foreign boats from transporting goods produced in Brazil, which could then be sold directly in the other European states without Portuguese intermediation.

The new colony, which King Manuel named Vera Cruz and later Santa Cruz, did not arouse the same enthusiasm as Vasco da Gama's discovery of the sea route from Portugal to India in 1497. The Portuguese believed that Brazil was a large island and offered nothing very interesting apart from Indians adorned with feathers and strange birds, including macaws and large, colorful parrots.

The birds were so famous that some writers described the country as "Parrotland." The name "Brazil" began to be used in 1503, when people realized that the wealth of the New World lay in the pau brasil tree, which produced a red sap that was used for dyeing and very strong wood used to build ships and furniture.

In the first 30 years after discovering Brazil, the Portuguese did no more than explore the Brazilian coastline, collecting wood and exotic birds, without venturing into the interior. The first attempts to explore the coastal region were to construct a

system of *feitorias*, fortified warehouses already used on the African coasts, not only for the defense of the territory, but also for trade with the natives. Brazil was leased for three years to a consortium of traders from Lisbon, led by Fernão de Noronha. The consortium was granted a trading monopoly, and in exchange had to commission six ships a year to explore roughly 1,240 miles of coast in the New World. But the venture did not live up to expectations, and when the lease expired, the crown commenced explorations alone.

to the desire to systematically organize the new land.

30 bottom
John III (1502–1557) was king of Portugal from 1521 until his death. Famous for having introduced the Inquisition into his country, in 1540 he divided Brazil into captaincies and instituted a general government.

30–31 *Once they discovered the new land, the Portuguese defended it against attacks by other expanding colonial countries, including France, which with an expedition led by Nicolas Durand de Villegaignon, attempted between 1555 and 1567 to found "Antarctic France" in the Guanábara Bay, Rio de Janeiro.*

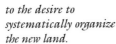

It was not until the Portuguese conquests were threatened by adventurers from other European countries (especially the French, who refused to recognize the Treaty of Tordesillas, founded some colonies, and indulged in piracy) that the Lusitanian crown began a full-scale policy of colonization. The first "colonist" was Martim Afonso de Sousa. He arrived in Brazil in 1530 with specific instructions: Expel the French and extend the Portuguese dominions by patrolling the coast. In the course of his duties, which he performed with great zeal and few scruples toward the local population, he founded São Vicente, where the first sugarcane was planted and cattle-rearing began. At about the same period John III, king of Portugal, divided Brazil into 15 parts, which were delineated by drawing a series of lines parallel to the equator from the coast to the Tordesillas meridian, and entrusted their management to 12 captains-in-chief from 1534 to 1536. The new governors of the colony came from a wide variety of social backgrounds, including minor nobility (those of high lineage were engaged in the more profitable trade with the Indies) and ordinary civil servants and traders, who had links of some kind with the crown and extensive powers in the economic, administrative, and legal fields. The experiment failed, with only two exceptions: the Capitania of São Vicente and that of Pernambuco.

In 1549, the crown tried a new strategy: Tomé de Sousa was named the first governor general of Brazil. He made his entrance to Salvador with a retinue of 1,000 people. Among them, as well as a small army, were Jesuits and Lusitanian prisoners. The task of the new governor was to colonize the country, while the Jesuits (among them were Manuel da Nóbrega and José da Anchieta, famous soldier-priests) were sent to "colonize souls"—in other words to convert the natives to Catholicism and turn them into "good Christians," devoted only to work (needless to say as slaves) and to the church.

Systematic colonization of the land and the native South Americans then began. The colonization effort included

33 left *Diamonds and gold mines were two of the new colony's major resources. In the regions of Bahia, Goiás in Mato Grosso, and especially Minas Gerais, the production of diamonds, emeralds, imperial topazes, aquamarines, amethysts, and gold reached incredible levels. The mines were a wonderful supplement for the waning Portuguese funds. The gold rush caused the first great wave of migration to Brazil, bringing approximately 600,000 people in the first 60 years of the 18th century.*

32 left
Tomé de Sousa, appointed first governor general of Brazil, arived in Salvador in 1549 with a following of more than 1,000 people. Accompanying him was the Jesuit Manuel da Nóbrega, accompanied by five brothers who wished to convert the Indians to Christianity and discipline the few priests in the colony. Father Manuel was a member of the conservative clergy and became famous for his definition of the Indians: "dogs who eat each other and kill, and pigs in their vices and relationships."

32 top right
The name of Bahia de Todos os Santos was given to the bay by the Portuguese sailors commanded by Amerigo Vespucci, who discovered this bay on November 1, 1502. The city of Salvador da Bahia de Todos os Santos (its full name) was built in 1549 under Tomé de Sousa. The baroque monuments date from 1600 when the city became rich as a result of the diamond mines discovered in the Chapada Diamantina, splendid canyons approximately 370 miles into the State of Bahia.

32 bottom right
Rio de Janeiro was founded on January 1, 1502, by André Gonçalves, a member of Amerigo Vespucci's leet. It was given this name because, to the eyes of the sailors, the huge Guanábara Bay looked like the mouth of a great river, the river of January. The Tamois Indians who lived along that stretch of coastline called the newly arrived people Cariocas ("white houses"), because once settled on land the Portuguese started to build brick houses that they painted white.

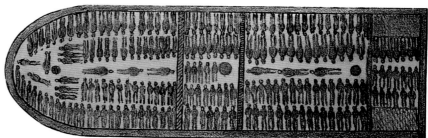

33 top right
The slave trade was extremely profitable; it has been estimated that between 1550 and 1885 more than 4,000,000 slaves, most of them young men, entered the ports of Brazil.

33 bottom right
Feitores, *armed with whips, kept a close watch over the slaves who used to wash the precious stones in the mines, as shown in this 18th-century watercolor in the National Library of Rio de Janeiro.*

agriculture; immigration by Portuguese colonists, the underprivileged, and convicts; and unrestricted use of slaves, first Indians (who cost a third of the price of African slaves), and then Africans, bought or captured on the coasts of Guinea, Congo, and Angola. At the same time Brazil's population was divided into "pure" and "impure" groups. The former were Portuguese citizens who were entitled to hold government office, receive titles, and so forth. The second group, called "new Christians," included everyone else: the Negroes, even if freed; Indians; and numerous types of half-castes. This distinction was abolished on paper by legislation passed in 1773.

The French and Spanish continued their raids until the early 17th century. The French founded Francia Antártica at Guanábara (Rio de Janeiro) between 1555 and 1567 and occupied the State of Maranhão, in the northeast of the country, between 1612 and 1615. Toward the end of the 16th century, the Dutch arrived on the Brazilian coasts and developed major interests in the country: They controlled 60% of the maritime trade in sugar between Portugal and Brazil, and 25 refineries in Amsterdam refined sugar imported from Brazil. In 1624, the Dutch attacked Salvador, the headquarters of the Portuguese central government but capitulated their new position the following year. The Dutch also held a coastal strip in the northeast for 24 years. This series of occupations gave rise to the creation of the *quilombos,* fortified villages inhabited by African slaves who had escaped from the plantations. The

34 *This map by Bleau shows the* capitanias *of Paraíba and Rio Grande. The drawings on top left and right show the conditions of local life at that time: a procession of Indians and a house perhaps near Pernambuco.*

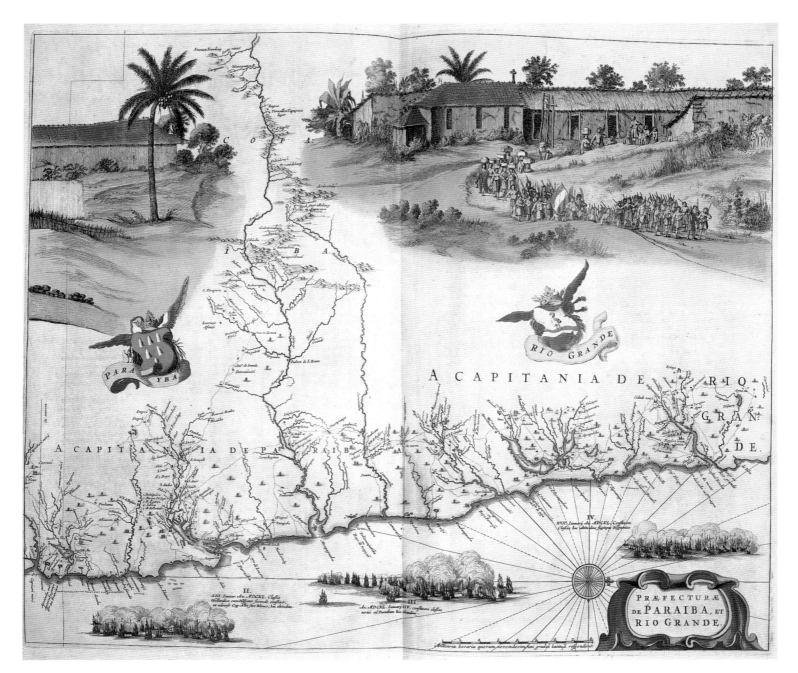

most famous quilombo was called Palmares.

Spain, France, and Holland refused to recognize the Treaty of Tordesillas, and the Portuguese Brazilians also refused to abide by the treaty rules. They organized numerous raids, called *entradas* or *bandeiras*, into the interior of the country, beyond the famous 370-league strip. Entradas were official explorations ordered by the crown and designed to consolidate Portuguese rule and fight the native rebels. Bandeiras were privately organized expeditions, mainly by inhabitants of São Paulo, to imprison natives for use as slaves and to prospect for gem deposits. The most famous of all the bandeirantes, Antônio Raposo Tavares, traveled 7,440 miles; he set off from São Paulo and reached Mato Grosso do Sul, Mato Grosso, Rondônia, and Pará.

35 top left
From the time of its discovery, Rio de Janeiro has been known for its mountains and above all for Pão de Açúcar, sugarloaf, still Brazil's best-known view.

35 bottom left
Pernambuco in an early 17th-century atlas by W. Blaeu. Recife, the capital, and nearby Olinda were embellished with splendid baroque monuments by the prince of Nassau.

35 right
This map of Brazil by Joan Bleau draws its inspiration from a map bought by Willem Blaeu in 1629. It illustrates Brazil in 1642, when the Dutch were trying to colonize a part of the east coast of the country.

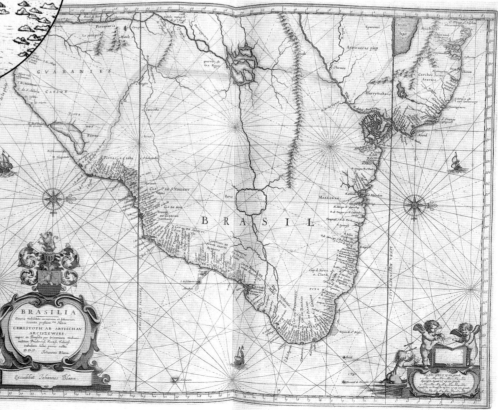

36–37 *An 1826 treaty allowed Britain to inspect Brazilian ships. This led to the sequestration of many slave ships. In 1850, the Brazilian parliament passed a law outlawing the slave trade. The number of Africans entering Brazil fell from 23,000 in 1850 to 3,300 just a year later.*

36 top left
José da Silva Xavier, known as Tiradentes, standard-bearer in the Dragoons of Vila Rica regiment (Ouro Prêto) was hanged and quartered on April 21, 1792. His limbs were hung out in the main Brazilian cities as a warning.

36 top right
Coffee, tobacco, and sugarcane, Brazil's main agricultural crops, occupied thousands of slaves. "Brazil is coffee and coffee is black" held the champions of slavery in the 19th century.

37 top
Slavery in Brazil witnessed epic rebellions by the slaves. The mythical Quilombo dos Palmares in the State of Alagoas provided a home to 3,000 runaways. The community was destroyed by a bandeirante, Domingo Jorge Velho, who killed the leader, Zumbí.

37 bottom
In 1835, hundreds of black Africans, slaves, and Moslem freedmen rebelled against slavery in Salvador. More than 500 Africans were killed. The revolt was called mâles, *after the Moslem slaves, but it was an isolated case. In Rio de Janeiro, where slaves amounted to 40% of the population, there were no uprisings. Harsh repression, the hope of gaining freedom, and different conditions of slavery for freedmen, slaves, Creoles, and blacks worked against a common rebellion.*

At the beginning of the 18th century, Portugal lost its role as a European superpower, and in 1711, signed the Treaty of Methuen with England, which placed the Lusitanians in a position of economic dependence and allowed the entry of English textiles into Lusitanian territory. At the same time, Brazil was growing increasingly aware of being a state, separated from Portugal not only by the Atlantic Ocean, but also by very different customs and lifestyles. In the second half of the 18th century, the American Revolution, the French Revolution (1789), and the beginnings of the English industrial revolution in Europe galvanized the attention of the new Latin population, especially the inhabitants of São Paulo and Minas Gerais, the two wealthiest and most culturally dynamic states. Independence movements flourished, such as Inconfidência Mineira (which demanded a republic modeled after the United States), led by dentist José Joaquim da Silva Xavier, known as "Tiradentes" (tooth-puller). Tiradentes was eventually betrayed, tried, and condemned, in a judgment that took the judges 18 hours to read, then hanged, drawn, and quartered. His head was taken to Ouro Prêto, then the capital of Minas Gerais, and displayed in the main square.

Another revolt by artisans, mainly mulattos and freed black slaves, was called the Revolt dos Alfaiates ("the tailors' revolt") because tailors joined the movement. The rebels demanded a republic, an end to slavery, free trade (especially with France), and an increase in soldiers' pay. This rebellion was also firmly put down.

Then, in 1807, ousted by the unstoppable advance of Napoléon's army, the Portuguese court hastily moved to Brazil. Between November 25 and 27 that year, 15,000 people embarked for the colony under the protection of the British army.

King John VI rewarded the British for their help by opening the Brazilian ports to them. The court settled in Rio de Janeiro. John conquered Uruguay, and in 1808 the first printed newspaper was published in Brazil and the kingdom's first bank, Banco do Brasil, opened. Rio became a major cultural center, with theaters, libraries, and literary and scientific academies. During the period of the king's residence, the population of the capital doubled, from 50,000 to 100,000. Many of the new residents were Portuguese, Spanish, French, and English immigrants, who formed a middle class of small businessmen and skilled craftsmen.

38 bottom right
The embarkation of the Brazilian troops at Grande Beach for the war against Uruguay in 1816. During that war, which was authorized by John VI, the Brazilians allied with Argentina.

38 left
John VI (1767–1826) was appointed prince regent of Portugal in 1792, when his mother, Maria I, was declared insane. He allied with Britain during the Napoleonic Wars, and, when the French troops invaded Portugal in 1807, he took refuge with his entire court of

scientists, artists, and intellectuals in Brazil. He was declared king in 1816 after his mother's death. The ceremony was celebrated in Rio de Janeiro.

38 top right
This gold coin, dating from the reign of John V of Braganza, king of Portugal, was

commonly used in the viceroyalty of Brazil from 1714. The coin's gold came from the gold mines of the southern regions.

38 center right
This 1839 engraving by J.B. Debret shows the acclamation of King John VI in Rio de Janeiro.

The Portuguese revolution of 1820 and the consequent repercussions in Brazil persuaded John VI to embark for Europe in April 1821, accompanied by 4,000 Portuguese. His son Pedro stayed in Brazil. Pressure for independence from a pro-Brazil faction steadily increased, and on January 9, 1822, Prince Pedro announced his decision to remain in Rio in the famous speech that began "Tell the people I'm here to stay." The date is still known to Brazilians ever after as *o dia do fico* ("I'm here to stay day"). The country had finally severed its links with Portugal.

On September 7, 1822, on the Ipiranga River, Pedro declared the colony independent, and at the age of only 24, he became Pedro I,

emperor of Brazil. In 1824, the first constitution was introduced, guaranteeing a hereditary constitutional monarchy. Legislative power was divided between the Chamber of Deputies and the Senate, and the country was divided into provinces, whose presidents were appointed by the emperor. In 1825, Portugal recognized the independence of Brazil, but as compensation for the loss of the colony claimed damages amounting to 2 million libras and an agreement not to persuade other Portuguese possessions to declare independence.

40 *Pedro II (1825–1891) was emperor of Brazil from 1831, the year his father, Pedro I, fled to Portugal, until 1889, when Brazil was proclaimed a republic and Pedro II himself was exiled to France. Slavery was abolished during his reign.*

41 top left *Giuseppe Garibaldi (1807–1882) supported the Farrapos Rebellion in Rio Grande do Sul (1839–1841). The rebellion was so named because the* farrapos, *or wretches, joined forces with the rich landowners. During those years, Garibaldi met and married the Brazilian Anita.*

The reign of Pedro I, first emperor of independent Brazil, lasted until April 7, 1831, when he was forced to abdicate in favor of his son, Pedro II. The king's abdications was the result of many causes: secessionist rebellions; a failed and expensive war with the United Provinces of la Plata (the future Argentina); the continually falling prices of coffee, hides, cocoa, tobacco, and sugar (at a time when the sugar market was already facing a crisis because of the entry of Cuba, a major cane producer, into world markets); the crisis of the Banco do Brasil; and the minting of easily counterfeited copper coins, all of which plunged Brazil into an economic depression.

Pedro II's accession marked the beginning of one of the most tumultuous periods in Brazil's history. Revolts in the north and northeast and the Revolta dos Farrapos (the Beggars' Revolt) in Rio Grande do Sul characterized the years until 1840. He stayed in power until 1889. During Pedro II's reign, slavery was banned (Lei Àurea, 1888) under pressure from the British, who had been calling for its abolition for years. Brazil's economy, which was based on the cultivation of coffee and rubber in the Amazon basin, flourished. Coffee accounted for

41 bottom left
The photo shows the funeral of Pedro II, who died in exile in France in 1891. Pedro's reign passed without bloody revolts and made way for the new republic.

41 right
The Àurea law (the original text is in the National History Museum in Rio de Janeiro) of May 13, 1888, officially abolished slavery in Brazil.

42 top left
Cangueiros Indians carrying a heavy barrel. This is a print by Jean Debret.

42 bottom left
The sugar industry was central to the social and economic life of the Brazilian northeast, Pernambuco, and Bahia.

42 top left
In the 10 years between 1870 and 1880, coffee represented 63% of the total value of Brazilian exports. The percentage climbed to 78% in the 1920s .

42 center left
Coal and corn merchants in an 1834 print conserved in the National Library of Rio de Janeiro.

52.7% and coffee for 25.7% of exports.

In 1891, the new republican constitution, which was based on the U.S. constitution, was passed, and the first waves of immigration from Europe began to arrive. Almost 4 million people entered Brazil between 1887 and 1930. But the period of greatest immigration was between 1887 and 1914, when 2,740,000 people landed in the country (72% of the total). The immigrants settled in the center-south, south, and east of Brazil. The State of São Paulo had the highest number of resident foreigners— 52.4%.

The end of the monarchy also led to the development of new power bases within the state. One of the strongest groups was the military, whose power reached its peak 80 years later with the 20-year-long dictatorship (1964–1984). The military came from the lower middle

classes, from the developing bourgeoisie that was soon to dominate the country, initiating revolts and upholding their rights against the landowners' oligarchy.

42 bottom right
Sugarcane was one of the first crops introduced to Brazil. The Dutch financed the production of Brazilian sugar.

42 *Gold mining on Itacolomy, the mountain shaped like a curved Indian woman, that dominates Ouro Préto, in Minas Gerais, made the fortune for this city.*

44 top left
President Washington Luís (left) poses with Herbert Hoover in Rio de Janeiro in 1929.

44 bottom left
Júlio Prestes won the elections of March 1, 1930. He soon had to face an opposition led by Getúlio Vargas, the future president-dictator of Brazil.

Brazil's central government was dominated by the two most economically powerful states, São Paulo and Minas Gerais. The First Republic was based on the principle known as *café com leite,* whereby a president of the Republic from São Paulo alternated with one from Minas Gerais. President Washington Luís broke with this tradition in 1929, when he named as his successor Júlio Prestes from São Paulo, who was elected in 1930. But the nomination was not accepted by either

Minas Gerais or Rio Grande do Sul, and on October 3, 1930, the spark of revolution flared, again with the support of the military. In a fortnight the army took control of the country, and appointed Getúlio Vargas provisional president of the new republic. The coup deposed the old coffee barons, strengthened central power, and allowed the rise of reformist sectors of the lower-middle class from which Vargas himself hailed.

Getúlio Vargas was one of the most interesting politicians in 20th-century Brazil. He came from south Brazil, of farming stock, and followed the classic political career, climbing all the rungs of the ladder to power. He remained at the helm of the country for 25 years. His policy was based on nationalism and populism, and he was very popular with Brazilians because he guaranteed a minimum wage, a social security system, state schools, libraries, medical assistance, and maternity leave. Trade unions were legalized,

44 top right
Getúlio Vargas made a triumphant entry to Rio de Janeiro and the rebellion died down. On November 11 a huge crowd filled the streets of Rio, sacking and burning the headquarters of the newspapers bound to the Prestes government, such as A Notiça in Avenida Rio Branco. This was the last act of the revolution.

44 bottom right
Salvador was left unscathed by the October revolution, when the rebels burned trams and blocked traffic in the streets near Branco River Park.

45 left
The revolution of October 1930 spread throughout Brazil, especially in the north, Paraíba, and Pernambuco, where the first sparks of rebellion exploded in March.

45 top right
Getúlio Vargas is received by high-ranking officers in Rio de Janeiro. The winner of the October revolution, for this occasion Vargas is wearing an elegant morning suit. Vargas started the long period of government that gave rise to the Estado Novo, a popular and nationalist dictatorship that lasted 25 years. Vargas's strategy was to conserve the support of the masses at all costs, and he succeeded by

proclaiming laws in favor of the workers, such as a minimum salary, a social-security system with paid holidays, maternity leave, and medical assistance.

45 center right
The rebel troops that made Getúlio Vargas president of the Republic enter Rio de Janeiro. The arrival of the "new man" was welcomed as the defeat of the hated oligarchy of landowners and coffee barons.

45 bottom right
Prior to its formal unveiling on October, 12, 1931, the statue of Christ the Redeemer attracted tourists in Rio de Janeiro. This photo shows British officers of the cruiser Dauntless *at the foot of the statue.*

although they were responsible to the federal government. The Roman Catholic church was a valuable ally to Vargas; from the time of the provisional government it guaranteed that the Catholic masses would support the state. In exchange, the government passed measures favorable to the church, such as allowing religion to be taught in state schools. The union between temporal and spiritual domains was symbolized by the statue of Christ erected in Rio de Janeiro. When it was inaugurated on October 12, 1931, Cardinal Leme consecrated the nation "to the sacred heart of Jesus, acknowledging Him always as its Lord and King." The provisional government ended with a

new constitution in 1934, and Vargas was elected full president of Brazil.

In 1937, claiming there was an imminent risk of a communist coup, Vargas, supported by the military, dissolved congress (which continued to represent a classist group), abolished the constitutional charter, and drafted another in which he was given almost absolute powers. Brazil entered the era of the Estado Novo and the years of dictatorship, which resembled the Fascist rule of Benito Mussolini. Like Italy, Brazil also had a propaganda ministry, the famous Departemento de Imprensa e Propaganda (Press and Propaganda Department), which was directly responsible to the president of the republic. Every day Brazilians had to endure the *Hora do Brasil* (Brazil Hour), a program that was later inherited by the military dictatorship and still exists today in democratic Brazil. Torture and exile were commonplace.

During World War II, the Estado Novo tried to maintain a neutral stance in the conflict between the Allies and the Axis powers. Later, under pressure from the United States, which had air bases in the north and northeast of Brazil in 1942, and as a result of huge demonstrations that called for Brazil to join the Allies, Vargas sent 25,000 Brazilian soldiers to fight with the U.S. Fifth Army in Italy. Four hundred fifty Brazilians died in the war, and they are

commemorated by a monument in Rio de Janeiro, on the Esplanada do Flamengo. After the Allied victory, the Fascist state headed by Vargas also came to an end, and in 1945 Vargas was deposed by the same soldiers who had helped him in his rise to power 15 years earlier.

power began to ebb. After a botched attempt by his followers to murder Maurício Lacerda, socialist leader of the opposition, the president, deciding that all was lost, shot himself in the heart on August 24, 1954.

Following Vargas's death, the last period of the Republic before the military dictatorship began. Juscelino Kubitschek from Minas Gerais was elected the new president. Although he encountered some difficulty in taking office (a military coup was required to install him, despite the fact that he was duly elected by the people—a unique case in the history of coups d'état), he based his policy on the Program of Goals. The program was designed to meet 31 targets

46 bottom right
Maurício Lacerda is greeted joyously in Rio de Janeiro at the end of the October revolution. Repeatedly imprisoned for his socialist ideas, Lacerda was the first to refer in Parliament to the new Labor Law code. Initially in harmony with Getúlio Vargas, he later became a sworn enemy of the dictator, so much so that men loyal to the president tried to kill him in 1954.

46 left
Eurico Gaspar Dutra (1885–1974) became general after bloodily repressing the 1932 Constitutionalist revolution in São Paulo. He also led the battle against the communist rebellion of 1935. Minister of war from 1936 to 1945 under Vargas, he organized the military forces sent to Italy with the Americans during World War II.

46 top right
Getúlio Vargas announces the members of the new cabinet in February 1951. Opposed by congress and other political forces, the old dictator began to decline, and on August 24, 1954, he committed suicide by shooting himself in the heart.

After Vargas was ousted, Eurico Gaspar Dutra, war minister under the dictator, was elected president. In 1946, another constitution was passed in which the country was defined as a federal republic and the president of the republic, elected directly by the people, was to hold office for five years. In the subtle world balance of the Cold War, Brazil, which now had very strong ties to the United States, acted as the South American bulwark against the threats of Communism and the populist trade unionism of Argentinian Juan Domingo Perón. The Communist Party was outlawed in Brazil, and American culture became increasingly dominant: Movie theaters showed only Hollywood films and the most popular magazine was *Reader's Digest*.

During the Dutra period, the indefatigable Getúlio Vargas prepared for his return, which was almost a foregone conclusion, on January 31, 1951. But congress and the opposition forces were hostile, and Vargas's

by the United States. Castro allied Cuba with the former Soviet Union, and fear of a Communist threat spread all over Central and South America. Jânio liked Castro, however, and he visited Cuba in 1960 and decorated another legend of the revolution, Ernesto Che Guevara, with the Ordem do Cruzeiro do Sul (Order of the Southern Cross), to the fury of the conservatives. Following accusations that he was planning a coup, Jânio was forced to resign on August 25, 1961.

47 top
Dwight D. Eisenhower visits Juscelino Kubitschek and is greeted in Rio by a cheering crowd in 1960.

47 bottom
Jânio Quadros da Silva (1917–1992) was elected president in October 1960.

divided into six major groups: energy, transport, food, basic industry, education, and the construction of Brasília, commissioned from the brilliant Oscár Niemeyer and Lúcio Costa. Brasília, called "the Goal that embraced all the others," was solemnly inaugurated on April 21, 1960.

In October of the same year Jânio Quadros da Silva was elected president. He governed in an unorthodox fashion, dealing with matters that were not strictly speaking the president's province; for example, he banned the *lança-perfume* (a canister, containing hallucinogenic substances, used at carnival time), bikinis on the beaches, and cockfighting. In 1959, the delicate Latin American balance was upset by the victory of Fidel Castro and his barbudos over dictator Fulgencio Batista, who was supported

48 top left
After four years of a fierce military dictatorship, Brazil exploded in 1968, but the student revolts were harshly repressed. The same year saw the birth of armed revolutionary groups against the government: *Aliança de Libertaçao Nacional di Carlos Marighella (killed by the military the* following year), the Movimento Revolucionário 8 de Otubro *(MR-8), and* Vanguarda Popular Revolucionária *(VPR), the latter with a strong leftist military component.*

The nomination of João Goulart, the vice-president who should by rights have taken office on Quadros' resignation, was suspended by the military, who considered him too liberal (Goulart happened to be making an official visit to China at the time). Some generals forbade his return to Brazil, while others supported him. The crisis almost led to civil war, but it was resolved when congress changed the system of government from presidential to parliamentary; Goulart remained in office, but he was subject to limitations.

48 right
Artur da Costa e Silva (1902–1969), soldier and politician, was elected president of Brazil by the National Congress (1967–1969) but was removed from office before the end of his term after he suffered a stroke.

48 bottom left
The student demonstrations continued, especially in Rio de Janeiro and São Paulo, and the police shot at body height, killing demonstrators. The students met in front of the American consulate to protest. After the uprisings in Brazil came *demonstrations in Chile and other Central American countries.*

But the peace didn't last long. In 1963, a national plebiscite called for the return of presidential government. Goulart regained full powers, promised social reforms, and threatened to nationalize foreign companies. Inflation, inherited from his predecessors, was sky-high, life was getting more expensive every day, and strikes and demonstrations were rife. On March 31, 1964, alleging that Goulart was planning a Communist coup, the military took over. Goulart fled to Uruguay, and for the fourth time since 1945, the army drastically interfered with the political life of Brazil. This last interference was to last the longest: 21 years.

In 1968, General Artur da Costa e Silva, successor of Castelo Branco, approved yet another new constitution. Protests by the young, who had witnessed the radical changes in Europe and the United States, together with acts of armed resistance, made the regime clamp down on opposition. The years of torture and exile that followed were the most tragic period in Brazilian history. Congress was closed down, and the government could arrest anyone without giving any reason. But the economy of the Latin American giant continued to grow, so much so that the economic boom of the 1970s was called Milagre Brasileiro (the Brazilian Miracle). The gross domestic product grew at an average rate of 11.2% per year, and inflation stood at 18%.

50 top left
*João Batista
Figueredo, the last
president appointed
with the support of
the military
dictatorship,*

*governed from 1979
to 1985. A general
and a politician, he
was in charge of the
São Paulo military
police in 1965.*

The economic boom came to an end in the 1980s. During the prosperity of the previous decade, deprivation of freedom and civil rights was ignored, but when the recession came, the issues moved to the forefront. João Batista Figueredo, who had promised to restore democracy, announced an amnesty for political prisoners and exiles; censorship was abolished, new parties were founded, and elections were held for governors and congress. But the return to freedom took place during a severe recession, when foreign debt reached the highest levels of the century. In January 1985, an electoral body formed by members of congress and the government appointed Tancredo Neves president, but he died shortly after the election. No one knows what really happened to the democratic

50 bottom left
*As early as 1983 the
Partido Trabalhista
was campaigning for
free elections. Street
demonstrations
called for* diretas já.
*On January 27,
1984, a massive
demonstration was
held in Praça da Sé
in São Paulo with the
participation of
thousands of people*

*demanding free
elections.
The same happened
in Rio de Janeiro.
The proposed new
Constitution, which
did not provide for
this type of vote
known as Emenda de
Oliveira, was rejected
by the Chamber of
Deputies by just 22
votes.*

50 right
*Tancredo Neves de
Almeida
(1910–1985) was
elected president of the
Republic by indirect
vote (by congress and
not by the people) on
January 15, 1985.
Tancredo was to be*

*invested on March
15. His supporters,
who had backed him
with demonstrations
all over Brazil, could
at last hope for a new
Brazil, but Tancredo
Neves never reached
the Planalto.*

Tancredo. After suddenly becoming ill, the president-elect underwent an emergency operation, oddly in the presence of politicians and friends. After another operation in São Paulo, Tancredo died on April 21, 1985, a symbolic date for the country because it marks the anniversary of the death of Tiradentes, hero of the Inconfidência.

At the Planalto (the Presidential Palace), Vice-President José Sarney took office. The recession absorbed the attention of the entire Sarney administration, which attempted to check inflation by introducing the Plano Cruzado and freezing prices, although wages were allowed to rise. The effect was a false boom that left the Brazilians with no savings, but Sarney was more popular then ever.

51 top left
José Sarney was the first nonmilitary president elected at the end of the dictatorship in 1985.

51 bottom left
On February 2, 1986, President José Sarney announced the application of the

Plano Cruzado. The old currency, the cruzeiro, was replaced the cruzado, in the proportion of 1,000 cruzeiros for 1 cruzado. Indexation was abolished, prices and exchange rates frozen, and the minimum salary was increased. The price

freeze was greeted with demonstrations in support of the president and with reckless spending.

51 right
In November 1982, after 17 years, more than 48,000,000 Brazilians voted to elect town councils

and state governors. The Partido Democrático Social (PDS), which was bound to the military, had to relinquish crucial positions such as governorship of the states of São Paulo, Minas Gerais, and Paraná.

In 1988, a new constitution was introduced (the last to date), and the northeastern politician who loved painting and literature remained in office until 1990, when the first democratic elections since the dictatorship were held. Brazil then went from the frying pan into the fire. By flaunting the most vulgar populism, a young politician from Alagoas, Fernando Collor de Mello (one of the 5% of the Brazilian population who own 95% of the country's wealth),

managed to get elected, beating Luís Inacío da Silva, known as "Lula," a former trade unionist and leader of the PT (the Workers' Party). The primary issues during the campaign were not political or economic issues, but an exchange of accusations and smear campaigns, aided by the television networks. It must be admitted that neither candidate was equal to governing a country like Brazil. But Collor, supported by the powerful Roberto Marinho, owner of Rede Globo, the largest TV network in Brazil, managed to win over the poorest classes, and defeated his rival by just a few votes. During the campaign, inflation rose to 1,700% a year.

The new president's first act after taking office was to freeze Brazilians'

53 left
Itamar Franco was appointed president when Fernando Collor de Mello, the first president of the Republic chosen directly by the people, had to abandon office because of a scandal unearthed by two journalists. Collor must be given credit for having started to improve the country's disastrous economic situation.

savings without any notice. He promised that this forced loan to the State would be repaid with interest in 18 months. Brazil plunged into a terrible recession; many businessmen suddenly found themselves with no money to pay wages or buy materials, and committed suicide, and the favelas grew to accommodate the new poor. Amid all this chaos two journalists (in an odd parallel of the Watergate scandal) discovered that Collor had embezzled money from the already impecunious

State of Brazil. His impeachment was inevitable, and huge demonstrations from Brasília to São Paulo forced the arrogant young president to leave the Planalto. He was succeeded by Vice-President Itamar Franco, who remained in office until the end of 1994. Franco was succeeded by Fernano Henrique Cardoso, a world-famous sociologist, professor at the Sorbonne, and former Labour Minster under Itamar Franco. Brazil's progressive politicians, including Lula, have been inspired by his books. Cardoso brought the runaway inflation under control, and when he was treasury minister in the previous government he introduced the Plano Real, as a result of which inflation plummeted from 150% a month to 2%.

53 right
Fernando Henrique Cardoso, a world-famous sociologist, is the current president of Brazil. Minister of the treasury under the government of Itamar Franco, he created the Plano Real, the new economic measures that, albeit with limits and adjustments, are leading Brazil to international economic strength. Although the constitution forbids the reelection of the president, a new law has authorized a second term for Cardoso so he can complete the work.

A GREEN HERITAGE

55 top
The jacaré (the caiman) can be found in the Pantanal, the Amazon, the northeast, and in some parts of the Central South. It can grow to 8 feet in length.

55 bottom
The ajaja ajaja is a type of flamingo found in swampy areas. During the mating season its back and neck are white, its chest and wings are pink, and its tail ocher-yellow.

54–55 *During Brazil's rainy season, which lasts from October to March, the rivers rise by as much as 10 feet. They flood their banks to form pools, where fish reproduce. Animals take refuge on the remaining patches of dry land. For the caimans this is feeding season. During the dry season they eat insects and small amphibians.*

54 top left
The Pantanal, a huge wetlands stretching for 88,800 square miles across the Mato Grosso, Mato Grosso do Sul, Paraguay, and Bolivia, is home to 600 different bird species, including the biguá (Phalacrocorax olivaceus).

54 top right
The Rhea americana, or emu, also lives in Brazil. It grows to a height of 4 feet and feeds on fruit, grain, and small animals. The male sits on as many as 40 eggs laid by different females.

The great Amazon rain forest occupies more than half of Brazil, but the country is vast and includes many other animal habitats. Scientists believe that one in 10 of the 1,400,000 species of living creatures in the world are to be found in Brazil. Of the 290,000 species of higher plants on Earth, 90,000 grow in Latin America, most of them in Brazil.

To convert these percentages into figures, the largest country in South America is home to 3,000 species of land-dwelling vertebrates, 3,000 species of freshwater fish, 55,000 species of flowering plants, 575 species of amphibians, 61 species of primates, 467 classified species of reptiles, and 1,622 bird species. Although many of these creatures live in the Amazon basin, the Pantanal, the huge swamp region, is also home to many animals.

The Pantanal (the name means swamp or marshland) basin is the remains of an inland sea that started to dry up 65 million years ago, during the Quaternary era. The sea was surrounded by tall peaks: the Serra de Maracaju to the east, the Bolivian Chaco to the west, and the Serra do Roncador to the north. The basin is in the middle of South America, is as large as France (88,800 square miles), and is shared by two Brazilian states (Mato Grosso and Mato Grosso do Sul), Paraguay, and Bolivia. Brazil houses just over half of it. Water, ever-present in the Pantanal, flows in small streams, rivers, ponds, and lakes, all of which intersect in an intricate navigable network.

The "Terra de Ninguem" ("No Man's Land"), as it is aptly nicknamed, is a paradise for bird-watchers and nature-lovers, who can observe 600 species of birds together with the ever-present *jacaré* (a type of alligator), crocodiles, iguanas, jaguars,

56–57
Praia do Forte is a fashionable seaside resort with a station for the observation and care of the sea turtles that flock to this coastline to lay their eggs.

56 top
Canoa Quebrada, 105 miles from Fortaleza, is a well-preserved fishing village. In the 1970s it was popular among hippies who came here seeking nature and a simple lifestyle.

deers, otters, giant and dwarf anteaters, monkeys, and tapirs. The water that fills the pools of the Pantanal flows down from the surrounding mountains, which are also the source of the Paraguay River that flows south into the Atlantic. The region can be visited only from April to September (you can make your base in the town of Cuiabá, on the border between the Amazon basin and the Pantanal). The rest of the year, during the rainy season, the area is practically flooded, the streams swell to rivers, and the dry land is reduced to islands called *cordilheiras,* where animals take refuge.

The Mata Atlântica is a huge forest that stretches from the northeast to Paraná, a state in the south of Brazil. This was the ancient forest encountered by the Portuguese colonists when they disembarked for the first time. The area is characterized by dense forest with a wealth of plant species, tall trees, and a wide variety of fauna, including parrots, toucans, and seagulls. It is also seriously endangered by the large conurbations that have developed over the centuries (especially São Paulo) and by the introduction of trees that have altered the bioclimate. At the cellulose factory at Ara Cruz, in the State of Espírito Santo, for example, eucalyptus was planted in huge quantities; this tree, which is used to make paper, absorbs so much water

that other plants are deprived of nourishment.

One of the best-preserved sections of the Mata Atlântica (the other is to the south of São Paulo, in the Vale do Ribeira, with 1,350 square miles of forest protected by a national park established in 1958) is the mountain chain called the Juréia (which means projecting tip in the Tupi-Guaranian language), a

58 top

The Aparados da Serra National Park stands on the boundary between the Rio Grande do Sul and Santa Catarina. This wide canyon, 150 miles from one extreme to the other, divides the two Brazilian states. Plunging 2,200 feet in some parts, it was created some 200 millon years ago by volcanic eruptions.

58 bottom

Mata Atlântica used to be a vast rain forest stretching from south Brazil to the northeast. Little remains of this huge green space that was once as big as the Amazon. Remnants of Mata Atlântica exist in the states of São Paulo and Rio de Janeiro.

huge massif that stretches down to the sea, on the São Paulo coast. It has 25 miles of unspoiled beaches, more than 400 species of medicinal plants, and hundreds of species of animals, especially birds, but it's only 124 miles from the chaotic São Paulo and 80 miles from Cubatão, a town known for its industrial pollution and illegal toxic waste dumps that have caused genetic defects in inhabitants, animals, and plants.

Before the national park was founded in 1987, the Juréia was threatened on several occasions. In the early 1970s, for example, Praia do Rio Verde, one of the loveliest beaches in the area, was nearly destroyed by a huge holiday resort. A few years later, in 1980, during the nuclear power boom, the president, General João Batista Figueredo, authorized the compulsory purchase of 90 square miles of land to build a nuclear power station; fortunately, the project attracted neither funds nor support. Perhaps because of these events, it is very difficult to enter the Juréia park today; visits by tourists are prohibited, and access is strictly limited to researchers and scientists.

In addition to the infinitely large Amazonia, the Pantanal, and the Mata Atlântica, Brazil is home to a seemingly infinite amount of wildlife. The Serra do Cipó National Park in Minas Gerais State contains the highest density of plants per square foot in the world; there are nearly 1,600 classified species (and researchers believe that a similar number still remain to be discovered) that flower year-round, continually transforming the landscape. Farther south, toward the Argentina border, dolphins and sea lions, which arrive punctually every year to escape the Antarctic winter, play under the huge cliffs of Torres, a famous holiday resort in Rio Grande do Sul. Hundreds of miles farther north, in the State of Bahia, whales gather every year to procreate and rear their young on the coast of Abrolhos. The name Abrolhos is a contraction of the phrase *"Abra los olhos"* ("keep your eyes peeled"), which is what sailors used to say when they ventured this way. They had to watch for the coral reefs called *cabeças,* impressive towers that rise up suddenly from the seabed to a height of 70 to 100 feet and upon which a ship can run aground. The archipelago, which consists of four main islands (Santa Barbara, Sueste, Redonda, and Guarita), was declared a national marine park in 1983.

Fernando de Noronha and Trindade, other islands off the Brazilian coast, have also been declared national parks. Fernando de Noronha is now a sophisticated resort, but only a limited number of people are allowed on the island

58–59 *Besides the vast plains, such as the Amazon basin and Pantanal, Brazil has mountains, deep hollows, and plateaus. Visconde de Mauá, a small town in the State of Rio de Janeiro, is a good example of the varied landscape.*

59 top *The Serra da Capivara National Park, in the State of Piauí, is protected by UNESCO. Twenty years ago Brazilian archaeologist Niéde Guidon discovered cave drawings and artifacts 48,500 years old in the park. So far, 363 archaeological sites have been opened in the Serra da Capivara.*

60–61 *Morro de São Paulo, 110 miles south of Salvador, is a popular tourist destination. The tranquil fishing village has been flanked by resorts and hotels that are gambling all on this still uncontaminated corner of paradise. The splendid beach overlooks the 16 islands of the federal district of Valença.*

62–63 *Of volcanic origin, these small islands just 10 square miles in all are an ideal habitat for turtles and the numerous fish species that live in the rocky crevices. Fernando de Noronha, the main island and the only one inhabited by people, is open only to organized tours. The number of visitors is limited to avoid harming the delicate natural equilibrium.*

63 top
The Abrolhos Archipelago, in the State of Bahia, like Fernando de Noronha, is a protected marine park. The whales of the Antarctic come to these warm waters to mate and spend the winter. The islands attracted Charles Darwin in 1832 and, much later,

the oceanographer Jacques Cousteau, who wanted to study the brain coral, so called because of its remarkable resemblance to the human organ. The archipelago's five islands are six hours by boat from the small town of Caravelas.

62 *The Fernando de Noronha Archipelago is a few hundred miles from the coast of Brazil in the Atlantic Ocean and is owned by the State of Pernambuco. In 1988, the 43 square miles became a marine park. The area was once a U.S. military base, then a jail for political prisoners under the military dictatorship.*

at any one time, and to ensure that only the right kind of tourist will visit, package prices are high. The first awed tourists, who flew from Vinha do Recife to Noronha in a military aircraft on December 7, 1972, were allowed into this Brazilian land, more than 186 miles from the coast, as a result of the expansionist policies of Brazil's military dictatorship. Fernando de Noronha Archipelago served as an U.S. base during World War II, and then a penal colony under the military dictatorship; it is now a protected marine oasis owned by the State of Pernambuco. These beautiful islands, which have a total area of 10 square miles, were discovered by Amerigo Vespucci in 1503. The 17 beaches of Fernando de Noronha, the main island, are reflected in a crystal-clear sea. The national park, which was created in 1988, includes the sea as well for a total area of 43 square miles. The scientists employed by the Tamar Project, an agency that protects and studies turtles, work here. Tourists who visit the area must adhere to strictly enforced rules; those who harm the wildlife on the archipelago are liable to expulsion. After years of neglect by man (goats were introduced and ruined the vegetation; huge lizards

called *teju* were imported to get rid of rats, but they preferred daintier fare such as turtles' eggs and birds), Fernando de Noronha is now a model for environmental protection projects in Brazil.

Trindade, the last outpost of Brazilian territory in the Atlantic, which lies 744 miles off the coast of the State of Espírito Santo, is also a protected area. The island, of volcanic origin, is at the far end of an underwater mountain range that starts on the coast of Espirito Santo and ends at Trindade. Like Fernando de Noronha, the island was a garrison (in World Wars I and II) and a penal colony. It has belonged to the Brazilian navy since 1957, and it is inhabited by 30 men who supervise the passage of ships and work in a meteorological center. Most civilians authorized to stay on the island are scientists working on the Tamar project. Trindade is a mecca for turtles, especially the green turtle, now very rare, which makes 6-foot-wide holes in the beach to house its eggs. Another of Trindade's highlights is the giant fern, which can grow to a height of 20 feet. For years these huge plants have been a mystery to botanists, who are unable to explain their origin.

CITIES SNATCHED FROM THE JUNGLE

RIO DE JANEIRO: MORE THAN A MYTH

64–65 *Ipanema and Leblon beaches in Rio de Janeiro. A road alongside the beaches links the Barra, the new residential district, to the center.*

64 top left
A cable car carries tourists to the top of Pão de Açúcar. From the summit the view sweeps the Corcovado, right opposite, the metropolis, and the morros, the hills that surround it.

64 top right
Leblon Beach lies just past Ipanema in the direction of Lagoa, and is known for the Morro Pico Dois, a hill with two peaks.

65 *At Rio's beaches, tourists and* Cariocas *alike strip off their clothes and spend some time in the sun, perhaps just for a game of beach volleyball or a half hour on the beach during their lunch break or at the end of the day.*

The 98-foot-tall Christ the Redeemer, anchored firmly on the top of the Corcovado, smiles down, arms outstretched toward Guanábara Bay and Pão de Açúcar (Sugarloaf Mountain). This is the most famous view in Brazil. The impressive stone and marble statue, donated by France and consecrated with full honors of church and state in 1931, during the dictatorship of Getúlio Vargas, has witnessed a great deal.

From the summit, Rio de Janeiro looks like a quiet, magical, inoffensive city, with a clear blue sea, a long bridge connecting it to Niterói, strips of sandy beach, and skyscrapers acting as a dividing line between the sea and the mountain. At the bottom is Avenida Vieira Souto, which runs along Ipanema, then Lagoa, São Conrado, the tunnel, and the Barra, the new Rio for the rich. The wind that blows on the Corcovado prevents any noise from reaching it. Rio is always bewitching from up here.

But the city can be a dangerous place. Between 1985 and 1991 there were 70,000 violent deaths in Rio, the same as the number of marines killed in Vietnam in seven years of war. The magic of one of the loveliest cities in the world risks being ruined when you walk along its streets. The people here are frightened; they live in fear of being robbed or killed for a few coins. Poverty and social inequality are rife in Rio, and more than a third of the 12 million inhabitants live in *favelas* (shantytowns). Murders of street children and shoot-outs between rival gangs of drug dealers are commonplace. Two tons of cocaine a month are consumed in this city, amounting to a turnover of $20 million.

Despite this terrible picture, which would suggest that a self-imposed curfew is advisable, the citizens of Rio (known as *Cariocas*), still go out on warm tropical nights. Rio is not only the birthplace of the samba and carnival, it is also home to culture and fashions, successful bands, and actors, singers, and authors. One reason for the large number of creative people in the city is that Rio is the headquarters of Rede Globo, the most important television network in Latin America. Roberto Marinho,

66 bottom
The beaches of Copacabana, Ipanema, Leblon, São Conrado, and now the Barra have made Rio de Janeiro famous. The Cariocas, as the inhabitants of Rio are known, live in

virtual symbiosis with the sand and sea—like the surfers who face the breakers of Guanábara Bay, heedless of the swimming ban signaled on many of the beaches fobecause of the high pollution levels.

67 *Sexual tourism has brought major income to the hotels and restaurants of Rio. Today, with the public campaigns promoted all over the country by*

Embratur, the Brazilian Ministry of Tourism, the pleasure seekers have left Rio and moved north to Recife and Fortaleza.

66 top
Rio's best hotels also stand along the crowded beaches of Rio —the mythical Copacabana Palace, the Othon, and the Caesar Park. Besides the beach and the calzadão, the black-and-white-tiled pavement, the city has numerous monuments dating from colonial and modern times.

66 center
Although not expressly banned, hardly any Brazilian women go topless. Breasts may be covered but not so buttocks, which many women prefer to leave bare.

the station's octogenarian owner, is the most powerful man in Brazil; he creates and destroys political careers, and decides who gets to be president of the republic.

Although Rio has not been the capital of Brazil for nearly 40 years, the beautiful, provocative Brazilian city still acts if it were—for better or worse. Apart from dancing, soccer is the all-consuming passion of the Cariocas. Imported by an Englishman in 1894, the game of bola is Brazil's favorite sport. At the legendary Maracanã Stadium everything is sacred, from the chair Pelé used to change and Zico's whirlpool to Garrincha's massage couch. Fetishism and iconoclasm are rife in the great stadium, which can hold almost 200,000 people. The walls are covered with photos of the stars who made the Brazilian team great: Rivelino, Junior, Zico, Garrincha, Romario and, of course, "o rei" (the king) Pelé, who is now minister of sport. Apart from Garrincha, who died an alcoholic, forgotten by fans and friends alike, the athletes made the most of the huge fortunes they accumulated. Artur Antunes Coimbra Zico opened a football school in the Barra and teaches the courses himself; Rivelino operates numerous junior football pitches in São Paulo, while Junior is a talent scout for the selectors and plays footvolley, a cross between football and beach volleyball, on the beach at Barra, in front of his house.

The beach is the common denominator in the city. The residents play, stroll, and make friends by the sea. At least once a day, early in the morning (rarely), during the lunch break, or at the end of the day, Copacabana, Ipanema, Leblon, and São Conrado fill with people. They sunbathe, have something to eat at the kiosks, or swim, despite the "No Swimming" signs. The beach is a way of life; it enables the Cariocas to have fun without spending much money and enhances their reputation as unenthusiastic workers.

Cariocas are deeply tanned and at the peak of fitness. Because they spend so much of their time in a bathing suit, their bodies must be presentable. This may be why Rio's college for plastic surgeons is the most famous in the world. Cariocas eat a healthy diet: big salads, not much meat, brown rice, fish, and plenty of fruit juice. Their diet always includes beer, a concession that everyone makes, whether they are dieting or in great shape.

Tourists who flock to the beaches and the five-star hotels often get caught up in the beach life. As a result, by the end of their trip, the vast majority know only their own hotel room, the beach, and a few nightclubs. Few tourists realize that one of the best collections of modern buildings in Latin America is hidden away in the oldest part of what was once the capital of Brazil. Nor do they know that the

68–69 *Corcovado, the mountain with the statue of Christ the Redeemer, has one of the loveliest sunset views over Guanábara Bay. The top can be reached by car, passing through the Tijuca Forest, or on a cog train.*

68 top
Rio de Janeiro is the most popular city in Brazil. More than 45% of tourists to Brazil visit Rio.

city government's Corredor Cultural, a walk through the architecture of an unusual Rio, which passes from the beautiful colonial style of the Paço Imperial (the Emperor's Palace) to Cinêlandia (the modern district where the city's movie theaters were built), from Confeitaria Colombo (a magnificent Art Nouveau building where hundreds of valuable glasses are displayed in the tall cases surrounding the bar) to the conical modern cathedral, and from the arched aqueduct, where trams now run, to the Municipal Theater, built at the turn of the century in the style of the Paris Opera House.

Even the Rocinha, the most famous of the 600 favelas on the hillsides around the city, has its own architectural style. It has now become a city within a city; buses run here, every home has water and electricity, and the colorful houses, seen from a distance, look like an Impressionist

painting. The Rio of the poor, for decades the symbol of abject poverty, is regaining stature; because of its location, which has a beautiful view of the city, real estate in the favela is now in demand. The inhabitants of the favela are well aware of this, and anyone wanting to buy land to build a house here has to pay a high city-center price for it.

69 *Rocinha is the most densely populated* favela *in Rio de Janeiro. Rocinha is a city within a city: It has more than a half-million inhabitants and its own bus service, electricity, and water.*

THE METROPOLITAN CONTRADICTIONS OF SÃO PAULO

70–71 *The Hotel Hilton skyscraper is one of the most modern skyscrapers in São Paulo and can be admired from the panoramic terrace of the Edifício Itália, the tallest building in the historic center.*

70 top left
Pedro I declared the independence of Brazil from Portugal in 1822 on the spot where the Ipiranga Museum now stands. Built in neoclassical style the museum houses objects that belonged to the royal family as well as the famous painting O Grito Ipiranga, which portrays Pedro I crying "Independence or death."

70 top right
The Bandeiras Monument stands in Ibirapuera Park, the large park of São Paulo. The bandeirantes *(flag wavers) were pioneers who joined together under the same flag to seek gold, capture slaves, and build new towns.*

71 *The Sé is São Paulo's modern cathedral and dates from the beginning of the century. The square of the same name, entirely shaded by majestic trees, is where the street children live and is one of the most dangerous parts of the city.*

long the Marginal Pinheiros, the orbital motorway that, with the Tietê, encircles São Paulo, are ultramodern skyscrapers, large shopping centers, residential complexes, and the World Trade Center. Then the *favelas* appear—shacks of cardboard and sheet metal that cover the natural undulations of the land. Behind them are the skyscrapers of Morumbí, one of the most fashionable and expensive districts of the city, where each apartment has a private swimming pool. The road continues with the alternation of opulence and poverty so typical of Brazil, interrupted by apartment buildings. The buildings are part of the Singapura Project, a face-lift operation ordered by Paulo Maluf, former mayor of the city. Eliminating the awful cardboard shacks, giving a home to the homeless, and introducing a semblance of cleanliness and decency to São Paulo was one of the priorities of his administration.

Expressing an opinion about São Paulo, the largest city in Latin America and second-largest in the world after Mexico City in terms of population, is a difficult task. At first sight, when you see the endless stretch of houses, skyscrapers, and favelas followed by more houses, skyscrapers, and favelas from the windows of the plane or the roof of the Edifício Itália, the tallest skyscraper in the city, your opinion is bound to be unfavorable. São Paulo looks like a jumble of buildings with no town planning and no shape. Then, as you explore the city, you discover that the chaos is actually an age-old order that cannot be altered. You realize then that the Brazilian metropolis is not a single city, but a group of towns, large and small, and that there is no single dominant culture (as there is in Salvador, where African culture predominates) but a number of cultures: Italian, Japanese, Lithuanian, and Arabian.

Going to Bixiga or Moca, the Italian districts, is nothing like entering the streets of Liberdade, the nearby Japanese district. There, red archways welcome visitors, and bilingual labels (in Japanese and Portuguese) on the products sold in the shops and on restaurant menus is common practice. The original cultures are manifested in the street decor, food, and cafés, as well as in the

language. The Festival of Nossa Senhora da Aquiropita, the Madonna who protects Bixiga, during the second week in August, is well worth seeing: Colorful stalls flying Italian flags sell pizza, lasagna, pasta, and sandwiches filled with calabreza, a spicy sausage, all of which is washed down with mulled wine.

What makes São Paulo interesting is the people who live there. According to IBGE (the Institute of Statistical Geography) there are 16 million people in the city, not including those who arrive every day in search of work and end up by swelling the population of the favelas. As many as 19 to 20 million people live in the metropolitan district of São Paulo. The neighboring towns no longer exist; they've been swallowed up by the inexorable advance of the capital. There are never enough roads; they disappear under the Pinheiros River, then climb to a viaduct and cross the river from the other side; favelas are razed and new bypasses opened to relieve the gridlock along the 62-mile route connecting one side of the city to the other.

Near Ibirapuera Park, in the southern part of town and São Paulo's largest park, stands a Formula One car. The stylized bronze vehicle, flying a flag, commemorates the victories of an unforgettable race-car driver from São Paulo named Ayrton Senna. The tunnel under the obelisk, which commemorates the martyrs of the 1932 revolution, is named after him. Designed by world-famous landscape gardener Roberto Burle-Marx, Ibirapuera Park is the meeting place for all the inhabitants of São Paulo; they flock there to eat ice cream, jog, sunbathe, admire the Japanese garden, and watch the blue herons in the great lake. Those lucky enough to live near the park are sitting on a goldmine; building is now prohibited in the area, and the skyscrapers built on the tiny spaces available (the land is exploited to the full) overlook the huge villas surrounding the park.

The city center, Praça da Sé (the cathedral square), is just the opposite of Ibirapuera. This is São Paulo at its noisiest and most irreverent. It attracts all sorts: The poor, street children who bathe in the fountain built above the subway, *camelô* (hawkers who sell strange potions), painters, and former hippies all flock here and to the nearby Praça da República to sell their homemade products. The pews in the cathedral serve as beds for the poor. During a service in the great church, the priest sings and dances to the rhythm of the music and the congregation follow his lead, while an army of children, adults, and senior citizens sleep stretched out on the pews or doze

72-73 *São Paulo measures 37 miles from north to south and the same from east to west. The exact number of inhabitants is unknown, but the number is thought to be more than 15,000,000 people, 10 percent of the national population.*

73 top *Every weekend the Paulistanos move to the beaches of Guarujá, a seaside resort 60 miles north of São Paulo. The litoral norte, of which Guarujá is a part, is one of the most beautiful coastlines in Brazil.*

behind the great columns, their few pathetic possessions done up in ragged bundles.

Light years separate these everyday scenes from Avenida Paulista, the best-known thoroughfare in the city. This is the financial center of São Paulo, where skyscrapers designed by world-famous architects reflect the opulence of what seems like a different city. Halfway along the avenue is the Rede Globo radio tower, which looks like a miniature Eiffel Tower at night. Also noteworthy are the Fiat Building and the MASP (Art Museum), designed by the Italian architects Lina Bo Bardi and Pietro Maria Bardi.

São Paulo's art and culture are housed in the Memorial da América Latina (a huge arts complex containing libraries, museums, and a theater and built by Oscár Niemeyer), the Municipal Theater, and the university, which has its own mayor who ministers to the continual needs of the huge American-style campus.

São Paulo never ceases to amaze the visitor. While Rio, with its legendary beaches, has remained unchanged for years, and Bahia lives on Candomblé, magic, and colonial buildings, São Paulo is the symbol of change, the metronome beating out the rhythm of this young country's growth.

This is perhaps the only way that the gigantic metropolis can convey to the eyes of the visitor something other than concrete, pollution, and contradictions.

74-75 *The obelisk-mausoleum in front of Ibirapuera Park commemorates members of the 1932 constitutionalist movement who died in the civil war that same year. The movement wanted the authoritarian Vargas to introduce democratic rule and was supported by the Paulistanos alone after Rio de Janeiro, Minas Gerais, and Rio Grande do Sul decided* to support Vargas, who was elected with their consent.

75 top
The Vale do Anhangabaú is a major road junction with tunnels that connect the south and the north of São Paulo. There is an excellent view of it from the viaduct of the same name that was built in the late 1920s.

SALVADOR, THE CALL OF MOTHER AFRICA

Today, like every Tuesday, is *o dia da bensa* (the Day of Benediction). The service is held at 6 p.m. at the Church of São Francisco. After mass, the celebrating monk blesses the congregation, numerous as ever, gathered in the shadows of the most famous church in Salvador, capital of the State of Bahia. Everyone attends the service: children and adults, rich and poor, and the sick, huddled on wheelchairs or leaning on improvised crutches. The time of devotion and meditation ends with the sign of the cross. Immediately after the prayer, the fun begins. The Pelourinho (the largest colonial city center in South America and protected by UNESCO) is closed to traffic, and the population throng the streets, drinking beer, chatting, dancing, and playing instruments until late into the night.

In the "Pelô" (as the Bahians affectionately call the Pelourinho), as in the rest of Salvador, even the smallest event is an opportunity for amusement. Up and down the streets the people go, laughing and dancing, talking and listening. In recent years, only the backdrop has changed. The old buildings, inhabited first by Portuguese noblemen and later by the homeless poor, were falling to pieces and have now been restored to their original splendor. This face-lift was ordered by Antônio Carlos Magalhães, former governor of the State of Bahia and one of the most influential politicians in Brazil. The result is astonishing to anyone who compares the faces of the Pelourinho before and after its renovation. Sadly, Bahians no longer live in the city center, which is now home to shops, restaurants, and jewelers, all for tourists. But the inhabitants of Salvador still come here to chat, listen to music, and sit in the cafés or in front of the Amado Foundation in Largo do Pelourinho. There is a saying in Salvador that every day God sends is a festival, and the city lives by this maxim. With its baroque churches dedicated to Christian saints and its *terreiros di candomblé* (areas consecrated to African deities), the first capital of colonial Brazil is the repository of Brazilian religions, so it comes as no surprise that many events are cause for celebration.

In Salvador, the majority of the population is black, and the rest are mulatto. "Is there a white man, even the whitest of the whites, who does not have some black blood in his blue veins? Doesn't the blackest black man also have a drop of white blood in his African veins?" wondered author Jorge Amado, the bard and symbol of Bahia. The mixture of races has created the "pure, unrivalled beauty of the Cape Verde mulattoes, creatures out of a dream, a dream of love," concluded the elderly author in his dissertation on the origins of the Bahians. And African culture is very much a part of Salvador. From the Pelourinho to the areas higher up, where houses give

78–79 *The Pelourinho is the colonial city center of Salvador. Nominated a World Heritage Site, it can now be admired in all its splendor thanks to careful restoration. More than $50 million, all provided by the Bahian government, has been spent so far to restore this colonial monument.*

way to shantytowns, the African culture of Candomblé, with the Yoruba deities Olodum, Oxum and Oxossí, Axé and Oxalá, is part of everyday life. Wherever you go, to the seaside, to the Modelo Market (where you can find absolutely anything), or to the new part of town, among the inevitable skyscrapers of a continually changing country, the African deities live and breathe.

The full name of the city is Cidade de Salvador de Bahia de Todos os Santos (City of Salvador in Bahia of All Saints). And in the city, *pai de santo* (Candomblé priest) Jubiabá, the hero of Jorge Amado's novel of the same name, inevitably comes to mind (there's even a square in the Pelourinho named after him). Very old, black as coal, dried up, incredibly thin, and enveloped in a gown that fluttered like a flag in the ocean breeze, at his house in Morro de Capa Negro, on the mountain above Salvador, Jubiabá saw into everyone's soul, read the good and evil there, helped, and cured. Salvador bowed to his wisdom. Another famous character, this time historical rather than literary, was Mãe Menininha, the famous *mãe de santo* (Candomblé priestess). She was consulted by politicians and artists and was so famous that people came from all over Brazil to ask her for help and advice. The people of Salvador also remember Irmã Doce, an elderly nun

who, like Mother Teresa of Calcutta, founded hospitals and assistance posts for the poor. These are the personalities of Bahia, present-day saints who join the holy men and women from centuries ago who are buried in the baroque church. Yoruba saints are also venerated in the Catholic Church of Nossa Senhora do Rosario dos Pretos, in Largo do Pelourinho, where the last scene from the movie *Dona Flor and Her Two Husbands* was filmed.

Veneration and respect for the deities are matched by equal devotion to music and the arts. African rhythms pulse in Salvador, which is also home of Tropicalism, a historical movement of Brazilian musical culture that began in the 1970s and was led by Caetano Veloso, Gilberto Gil, and Gal Costa. Axé music (a blend of the music of the Olodum and Timbalada tribes), the romantic dance music of Daniela Mercury, and the eclectic sounds of Carlinhos Brown are also popular in Slavador. "The Americans had to build Disney World to have fun—Bahia was created like that," quips Daniela Mercury. There certainly is no lack of gaiety and love of celebration even among the poorest of Salvador's poor, who live in shantytowns by the sea or perched on the mountainside. Magic and fun, philosophy of life and tradition, Europe and Africa, the sacred and the profane—all are found in Bahia.

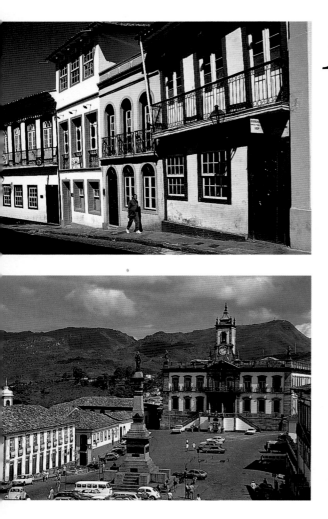

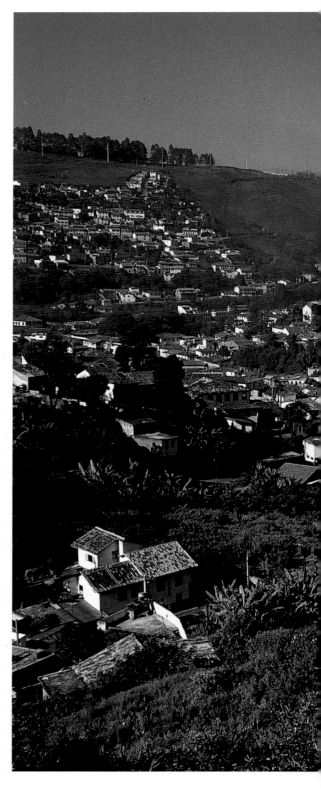

80 top
Ouro Prêto is a university town and home of one of the most prestigious mineralogy faculties in the world. The students live in repúblicas, *student-run houses where visitors can stay and students study, dance, and socialize.*

80 bottom
Praça Tiradentes is the main square of Ouro Prêto and divides the town in two parts. In 1792, the head of Joaquim da Silva Xavier, the leader of the Inconfidentes who called for the independence of the State of Minas Gerais from Portugal, was hung here.

Many people swear they have seen him at least once. In the Church of São Francisco de Assís, one of the most outstanding examples of colonial baroque architecture, a hooded friar wearing a black cloak slowly walks and prays, his habit brushing against the solid wooden pews. If anyone tries to approach him, he vanishes. The ghost of the praying Franciscan is just one of those who glide undisturbed and disappear among the majestic walls of Ouro Prêto, the ancient capital of Minas Gerais. Spirits and goblins haunt the quiet nights of the ancient Vila Rica (the city's original name). Some shuffle around the churches like Maria Chinela (literally Mary Slipper), a little old black lady who used to stroll along the streets of Vila Rica many years ago and now fills the Church of Nossa Senhora do Monte do Carmo with the sound of her shuffling footsteps. Others mourn their lost love in the cemeteries, like Bolão, an insensitive student who rejected his fiancée, Emília. She died of a broken heart, and he was found dead on her grave. Some speak the African Yoruba language in the churchyard of Santa Efigênia, the place of worship of the slaves, who fooled the Jesuits and the Portuguese by hiding symbols of their own deities among the Christian symbols. Others attend evening mass, shrouded in black cloaks, before returning to their tombs, as

80–81 *Ouro Prêto is situated on a mine of precious stones: aquamarines, topazes, and emeralds. Stone-cutting and setting have provided the town with its major source of income since 1750, when Ouro Prêto had more inhabitants than New York City.*

81 *São Francisco de Paula was the last church built in Ouro Prêto. Work on the cathedral ended at the beginning of this century. It stands in a privileged position at the top of a hill overlooking the lovely colonial city of Minas Gerais.*

82–83 *The Church Nosso Senhora do Monte dor Carmo, the work of Aleijadinho and his father, Manuel Francisco Lisboa, is marked by the absence of baroque decorations. There is no excess here, only harmony and simple design. The church is part of the third and last phase of Mineiro baroque style.*

82 top
Fountains are common in the streets of Ouro Prêto. In 1980, the town was placed under UNESCO protection.

once happened on a dark rainy night at the Church of Nossa Senhora das Mercês e Misericórdia. The comings and goings of ghosts and zombies is enough to terrify even the most sceptical of visitors.

Whether the stories are true or not, one thing's for sure: Ouro Prêto, a town nestled at the foot of Pico de Itacolomí, a mountain that resembles a bent old woman, does offer something special. Here religion blends with animist cults, popular beliefs with sacred places, and solemn buildings with the cheerful din made by students enrolled at one of the most famous universities in Latin America.

Gold, topazes, emeralds, aquamarines, and rubies made Ouro Prêto a fabulously wealthy city. In 1750, it had more inhabitants than New York City. In just over a century, between 1700 and 1820, some 1,200 tons of gold were mined in the State of Minas Gerais, accounting for 80% of world gold production. Ouro Prêto was the hub of mining activities. Chronicles of the period recount that even the slaves were dressed in gold. One of them, Chico Rei, an African sovereign deported with his whole tribe in the early 18th century to work in the mines, became a legend. Legend has it that by hiding gold dust in his hair, he managed to accumulate enough money to buy freedom for

his whole tribe and purchase a mine, Encardideira, which the Portuguese believed to be worked out. Chico struck a gold seam and became a rich and powerful man. To thank Efigênia, the Christian Nubian princess who was the patron saint of the tribe, Chico built a church named after her. A commemorative mass was celebrated on January 6 for many years. On that occasion the black women sprinkled gold dust on their heads and rinsed their hair in holy water after the service, thus contributing to the maintenance of the place of worship.

The saying that Ouro Prêto has more churches than houses may be exaggerated, but 13 churches and 6 chapels in one small town is certainly no small number of religious buildings. These places of worship were built in the golden years of the 18th century, when rich men and aristocrats, under pressure from the Jesuits, who admired baroque art, vied to erect the most magnificent building. The last *igreja* to be built was the Church of São Francisco de Paula, which was started in 1804 and finished exactly a century later, in 1904. More recently, the only construction in the city center was of a hotel built in the 1960s by architect Oscár Niemeyer. The all-concrete building is a fine example of "new style" design, but it is somewhat out of place.

83 top
São Francisco de Assís is perhaps the most outstanding work of António Francisco Lisboa, the architect and sculptor responsible for most of the monuments in Minas Gerais.

83 bottom
Inside the Church of São Francisco de Assís are paintings by Manuel da Costa Ataíde, one of Brazil's most famous painters who worked on the church from 1801 to 1812.

84–85 *The sanctuary of Senhor Bom Jesus de Matozinhos is the main attraction in Congonhas do Campos. Except for this baroque religious complex, the town remains fairly anonymous.*

84 top left
The imprisonment of Christ by Aleijadinho, a nickname that in Portuguese means "little cripple." The artist suffered from severe deforming arthritis and hid his body beneath a large cloak to hide his handicaps. Toward the end of his life, to continue sculpting, he had the hammer and chisel strapped to his hands.

84 top right
Sixty wooden statues make up the Way of the Cross in small chapels in front of the sanctuary of Congonhonas do Campos. The suffering Christ with almond-shaped eyes and mouth half open in a grimace of pain is perhaps the loveliest. All are the work of Aleijadinho.

The opulence was entrusted to the skillful hands of carpenters and craftsmen, working to the orders of a genius of church architecture, Antônio Francisco Lisboa, known as "l'Aleijadinho" ("the little cripple"). Many tales are told about this illegitimate son of Portuguese architect Manuel Francisco Lisboa and an African slave called Isabel. At age 47, the artist contracted rheumatoid arthritis. The disease twisted his body and crippled him. To hide from the eyes of people who remembered him as a dashing young man, he wore a large black cloak with a hood. During the last period of his life he is said to have had a hammer and chisel bound to the stumps of his arms so he could continue to carve. Aleijadinho designed São Francisco de Assís and many other churches in the city and left a series of magnificent statues in Minas Gerais, especially the 12 Old Testament prophets who adorn the facade of the Sanctuary of Senhor Bom Jesus de Matozinhos at Congonhas do Campo (Isaiah, the first on the left, small and bent with a pain-racked face, is a self-portrait of the artist) and the capitals of the Via Crucis, resembling life-size theater sets, in the same place. Antônio Francisco Lisboa hated the Portuguese, whom he regarded as invaders, as did all the intelligentsia of Minas Gerais. (Ouro Prêto was the center of the Inconfidentes conspiracy led by Tiradentes.) Aleijadinho's chisel was the ideal weapon to fight and denigrate the Portuguese. All his statues representing treacherous or evil characters were ugly portraits of Portuguese personalities. One example is the statue of São Jorge, housed in the city's museum. Aleijadinho resented the fact that Bernardo José Lorena, the Portuguese governor who commissioned him to carve a statue of St. George, had looked at his horribly deformed body with disgust. The artist had his revenge by giving the saint the features of the nobleman's servant, accentuating his physical defects, and intentionally botching the proportion between torso and legs. The result was that for many years, instead of ending with prayers and devotion, the procession of São Jorge dissolved into hilarity.

85 top
The prophet Isaiah is one of the 12 soapstone statues that adorn the stairway of the Church of Senhor Bom Jesus do Matozinhos in Congonhas do Campo. Experts believe that Isaiah is a self-portrait of Aleijadinho.

85 bottom
The statue of Ezekiel stands on the stairway of the Church of Senhor Bom Jesus. The religious complex has an unusual Way of the Cross by Aleijadinho.

BRASÍLIA,
AN IMPOSSIBLE DREAM

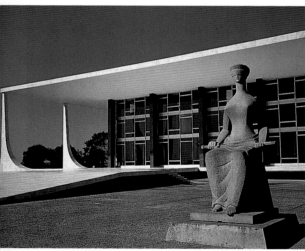

86 top
*Brasília
revolutionized
architecture.
Concrete was
fashioned with
simplicity, and the
city's beauty came
from the ensemble of
buildings and open
spaces.*

86 bottom
*In front of the
Supreme Court of
Brasília is the statue
symbolizing Justice,
blindfolded and with
a sword in her lap.
Most of the buildings
in Brazil's youngest
city were designed by
the architect Oscár
Niemeyer.*

A red cloud shrouds the blue sky above the city. It's a dust cloud, formed by the blood-red soil of Brazil, stirred up by the wind. This phenomenon occurs frequently in winter, when the humidity level can be as low as 18%–20%. This is the wild Planalto Central, at an altitude of 3,600 feet in the State of Goiás and the geographical center of Brazil. Thirty-seven years ago, this godforsaken spot was chosen as the birthplace of a city, or rather the city—Brasília, the capital, the first 20th-century metropolis to be built from scratch. The impressive project was designed by three famous names of modern architecture: town planner Lúcio Costa, architect Oscár Niemeyer, and landscape gardener Roberto Burle-Marx. Brasília was the first modern city to be classed by UNESCO as a "heritage of the human race."

"Architecture should be a manifestation of spirit, imagination and poetry," said Niemeyer when Brasília took shape. The new architectural style, which was daring and futuristic in the 1950s and 1960s, was used to construct the Education Ministry Building in Rio de Janeiro, the first building designed by the trio and their reference for Brasília. Despite their real artistic and innovative merits, the new designs did not produce a very functional city; in fact, Niemeyer himself admitted that the needs of sophisticated planning and structural studies took precedence over the convenience of residents. The identical blocks recall the depressing buildings of Communist countries, the streets have numbers instead of names, and the concrete can be oppressive. But the capital, which was designed to house 400,000 people, now has a population of 1,750,000. Many of them, especially the *candangos* (the pioneers who built Brasília) now live outside the city, in favelas that stretch as far as 19 miles from Plano Piloto, the project's first building. The other residents, nearly all of them civil servants who work for ministries or government agencies, live in low-rise buildings or pretty villas on the lakeside, the residential area. Brasília has a fluctuating population: It is overcrowded from Monday to Thursday and deserted on weekends, when members of congress, secretaries, bag-carriers, and civil servants return to their home towns. Those who can't afford the flight every weekend flock to private clubs out of town.

It was very difficult to populate the new capital. Forty years ago, to persuade civil servants and politicians to leave Rio de Janeiro, Juscelino Kubitschek appealed to their wallets, doubling their salaries. Now, 37 years later, more and more people live in this strange city, a work of art that belongs to "a different planet, not the earth," as astronaut Yuri Gagarin commented when he visited it for the first time.

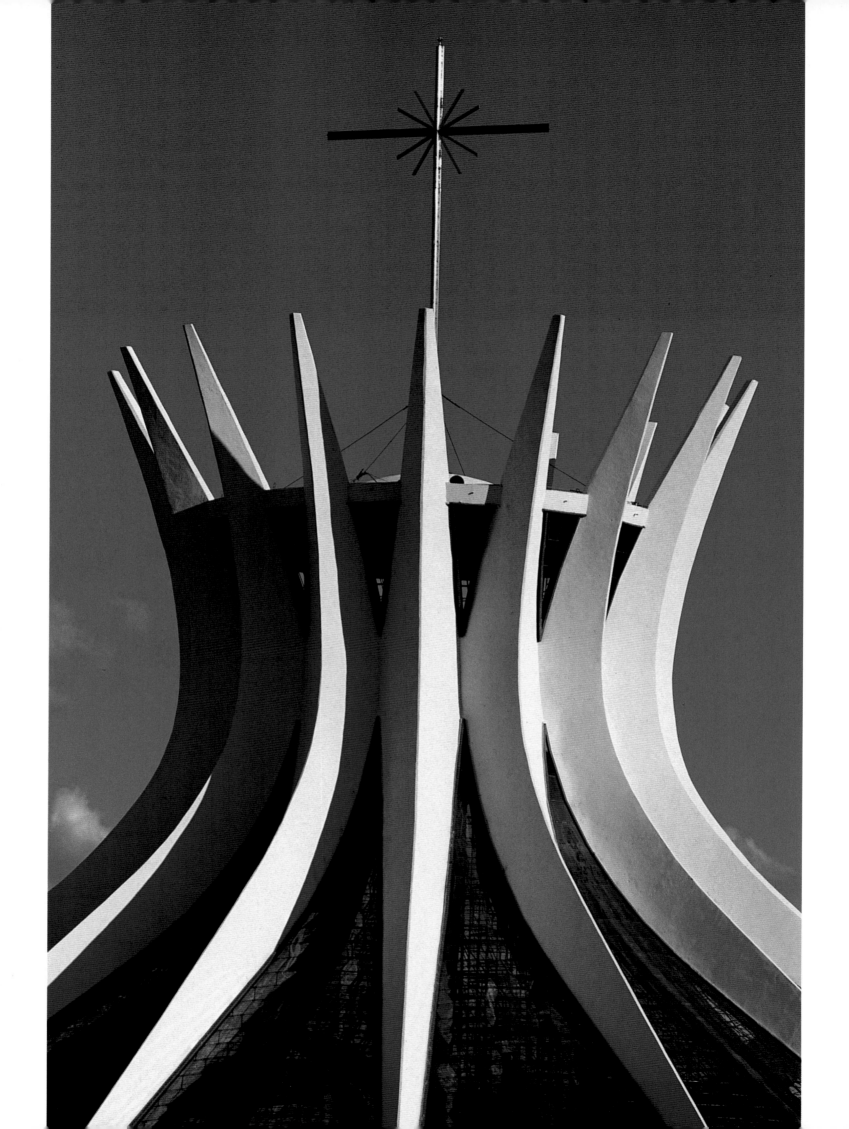

88 and 89
Brasília's cathedral is Niemeyer's greatest achievement. It was inaugurated in 1967, 12 years after work commenced. Conceived as a universal place of worship, it was consecrated to Catholicism and named *Metropolitana de Nossa Senhora Aparecida Cathedral. The building has a single nave supported on external pillars, and from above it looks like a flower* (center) *covered with glass windows that create a play of light and color inside. The entrance to this* *splendid modern church was designed as a journey of purification toward God: the doorway is in semidarkness and as the visitor proceeds toward the central nave the light becomes gradually brighter before exploding at the main altar* (bottom).

Brasília is certainly a world apart. A world influenced by many factors, from the school that developed in São Paulo after Modern Art Week was held there in 1922 (Niemeyer was only 13 at the time) to the arrival of architect Le Corbusier in Rio de Janeiro in 1931. Le Corbusier gave a clear direction to the work of young Brazilian architects, including Costa, Niemeyer, and Burle-Marx. Simple design, economical use of construction materials, and large open spaces—these were the lessons of the French master and the ideas that inspired the construction of Brasília.

The city not only represents the application of revolutionary tenets of style, it also incorporates a compendium of Brazilian philosophy. Everything in the city has a carefully designed symbolism. For example, the city is shaped like an airplane, with the Planalto (Presidential Palace) occupying the cockpit position, signifying that this new city, where the political and administrative heart of the country beats, will lead Brazil to the future and a better world. The magnificent cathedral, one of the most famous monuments of the 20th century, is also imbued with symbolism. Niemeyer intended the cathedral, inaugurated in 1967 after 12 years of work, to be an ecumenical religious center, a place of worship where all Brazilian religions would be equally welcome. But the place of worship was transformed into the Roman Catholic Metropolitana de Nossa Senhora Aparecida Cathedral. The circular nave is belowground and is reached by walking through a black tunnel that opens onto a softly lit room called the meditation area. After crossing this room, you reach the central nave, which is illuminated by natural light filtering through the stained-glass windows that form the walls. The journey is a kind of pilgrim's progress to God.

The buildings housing the ministries in the wide avenue named after them are all the same, and the street ends at the Square of the Three Powers: the executive represented by the Planalto, the judiciary by the Law Courts, and the legislature by the twin towers of the National Congress. On either side of the square stand the most important ministries—the Ministry of the Interior and the Itamaraty (Foreign Ministry)—a perfect harmony of concrete, tropical plants, and water cascading down the pillars of the buildings' facades to collect in a huge fountain. Niemeyer used the same elements in other buildings: the French Communist Party Building in Paris, the National University in Algiers, the Mondadori Building in Milan, and the Church of São Francisco de Assís, with frescoes by Cândido Portinari, in Pampulha, Belo Horizonte (Minas Gerais).

Parks and gardens, another important feature of Brasília's design, were

90–91 *It was difficult to populate Brasília. The first to arrive were the civil employees, who were abruptly wrenched away from the beauties of Rio and thrown into a city that had nothing in common with the Cariocan beaches and nightlife. Salaries were increased to encourage transfers but even now, on weekends, the residents take refuge in clubs outside the city or in villas around the artificial Paranoá Lake.*

The Esplanada dos Ministerios ends in the Praça dos Tres Poderes. The capital, designed for 400,000 people, today has 1,750,000 inhabitants. Many people work in the ministries and live in the city only from Monday to Thursday.

designed by Burle-Marx. Cidade Park covers an area of almost 2 square miles and has every kind of recreation, including bicycle paths, children's play areas, a lake with fishing, and a swimming pool with artificial waves. There's also a huge indoor area and a 1,400-seat amphitheater.

Brasília is an acquired taste. You learn to like it, or even love it, for its new, simple but complex forms. Alçeu Valencia, a singer-songwriter from the northeast, best expressed the story of Brasília, new capital and white elephant of Planalto Central, Gioás:

"Now I know your geography,
your soft skin, girl city,
your sex, your lake, your symmetry.
See you soon, I love you, Brasília."

91 top
Brasília, today a federal district, is actually part of the State of Goiás. The city lies in the geographical center of Brazil, in a desert area where humidity reaches only 15%. Often the sky is red, colored by the dust raised by the wind.

91 bottom
The monument to the candangos, the workers and natives who built Brasília, stands right in front of the Ministry of Justice. The candangos now live in shantytowns extending up to 20 miles outside the Plano Piloto, the original nucleus of the city.

92–93 *In Curitiba, the capital of Paraná, everything works like clockwork. But this perfect city has lost most of its magical South American atmosphere.*

93 top
Florianópolis is the capital of the State of Santa Catarina, an island in south Brazil. This unusual city, with a mild climate and European buildings, has 42 beaches.

93 center top
Recife, the capital of Pernambuco, in the Brazilian northeast, is also known as the Venice of Brazil because of its numerous bridges. Recife is experiencing the same problems as Fortaleza: large-scale tourism, social inequality, and child prostitution.

93 center bottom
Fortaleza, the capital of the State of Ceará, northeast Brazil, is a popular tourist destination.

93 bottom
The capital of Rio Grande do Sul, Brazil's southernmost state, Porto Alegre is the home of gauchos, the Brazilian cowboys. The economy of the state is based on cattle breeding in large fazendas.

94 top and bottom
Every inch of wall and ceiling of the Church of São Francisco de Assís in Salvador bears finely worked inlays covered with gold. Salvador, like the mining town of Ouro Prêto, has more churches than houses, all built to show the power of the wealthy businessmen and nobles. The places of worship used by the slaves are distinguished by their clean lines and simple interiors.

94–95 *The best time to admire the refined inlays in the the interior of São Francisco de Assís is during services, when the whole nave is illuminated.*

95 top
The facade of São Francisco de Assís in Salvador. To the left of the church is the Igreja da Ordem de São Francisco da Penitência, part of the same religious complex. The front is lined with statues and sculpted reliefs typical of Portuguese and Spanish baroque style.

96–97 *The Capela Dourada in Recife stands opposite the law courts. It can be visited every day between 8 and 11:30 a.m. and 2 and 5 p.m. Beside it is the Sacred Arts Museum, which has the same opening times.*

96 top left
*The Cathedral of
Nossa Senhora do
Pilar di São Joao del
Rei, Minas Gerais,
was built in 1721 and
displays a wealth of
azulejos and gilded
altars.*

96 top right
*The Capela Dourada
in Recife belongs to
the third Order of São
Francisco and stands
in the Santo Antônio
district. Built in
1692, the project is
attributed to Antonio
Fernandes de Matos.
The reliefs showing the
Virtues are the work
of Antônio Santiago.*

97 *The Church of
Nossa Senhora da
Conceição, Recife.*

BRAZIL'S DIVERSITY REVEALED

I t has taken 500 years to form the Brazilian population, which is made up of some 147 million people (according to the 1991 census, there will be 180 million people in Brazil by the year 2000) living in a huge territory of 32,864,696 square miles, an area more than twice the size of India. Although Brazil has the fifth-largest population in the world, it is one of the least populated countries, with only 51 inhabitants per square mile. This distribution is obviously an average; in practice, most of the population is concentrated in the large metropolitan areas. According to a survey by IBGE (the Brazilian Institute of Statistical Geography), 75% of Brazilian families live in urban areas. In the State of Rio de Janeiro, for example, 90% of the inhabitants live in towns, while in the State of São Paulo, the proportion is 88%. More than half the population of Brazil, some 80 million people, is concentrated in the southeast of the country; this area, which might be described as the most industrialized part of Brazil, occupies only 10.85% of the country's territory. Brazil also has the largest mixed-race population in the world.

So how was the Brazilian population formed? Many anthropologists agree that the first men to live in Latin American were people of Mongol origin who crossed the Bering Strait in the far northeast of the American continent after an ice age, probably pursuing animals fleeing

from the freezing cold. This happened 15,000–25,000 years before the arrival of Europeans on the continent. Some experts believe that the South American populations arrived not only from the Bering Strait but also from the south, from Polynesia and Australia, and that the native South Americans are a blend of the two races. Before the Portuguese arrived there were about 3 million Brazilian Indians in the country, descendants of the first immigrants in human history. After 500 years of colonization, compulsory and voluntary immigration, and dominations that have united Africans, Indians, Europeans, Arabs, Asians, and Caucasians, the indigenous population has been reduced to some 270,000, a

98 and 99 *Brazil is perhaps the only country on Earth to contain all the races of the world: native South Americans, the original inhabitants; Africans, present in massive numbers in the states of Minas Gerais and Bahia, who arrived as slaves; Europeans (Germans, French, Dutch, Spanish, Russians, and Italians); Arabs; Persians; Japanese; and Chinese. Despite the apparent calm between different races, Brazil is a classist society. Racism may not be visible, but it exists and is more a conflict of social standing than of skin color.*

number that may be overestimated. The history of Brazil's Indians is full of massacres, violence, and tyranny, and the Africans immigrants did not fare much better. Between 1531 and 1855 (when the slave trade was abolished), some 4 million Africans were deported to the new Portuguese colony. So many Africans were imported into Bahia, Pernambuco, Rio de Janeiro, Minas Gerais, and

Maranhão that the slave population outnumbered the free population. The colony's labor force came from the Gulf of Guinea, Angola, and Mozambique. Many African men came from Islamic areas with Arabic culture and language. Every African who arrived as a slave brought his own culture and preserved it jealously, handing it down from generation to generation. In addition to African slaves, Brazil received Asian immigrants: Chinese, Koreans, and Japanese. The Japanese began to arrive in the tropics in 1908. Organized in cooperatives, they specialized in producing and marketing fruit and vegetables and growing rice and tea. The largest number of European immigrants came from Italy, and these arrivals colonized the southern parts of the country.

Although cultures and races have blended in Brazil, racial rivalry still exists. Racism, especially toward blacks and Indians, did not die out with the abolition of slavery in the 19th century. Racial inequality is evident in the fact that the poor who live in the shantytowns are mainly blacks and northeasterners, close relations of the Indians. And the number of poor people in Brazil is staggering: In Rio de Janeiro, for example, one inhabitant in three lives in the favelas, while in Belo Horizonte, capital of the State of Minas Gerais, the proportion is one in four.

100 top
African influences appear in in religious rites, animist rituals, music, and dancing. The samba, the most famous Brazilian dance, comes from the African savannah. The cultural hotbed of music and dancing is Bahia, where 90% of the population is black or mulatto.

100 bottom
Gilberto Gil is one of Brazil's most famous musicians. Persecuted under the dictatorship, in the early 1970s, he and Caetano Veloso invented tropicalism, an artistic and cultural movement that has influenced Latin-American music for the past 30 years.

100-101 *The body-beautiful cult is strong in Brazil. Jewelery, cosmetics, and fitness are national obsessions.*

101 top
Candomblé, like voodoo a cult of Yoruba derivation, is the most widely followed religion in Salvador. Only followers can watch the ceremonies, although public rites are performed for tourists and to earn some money. In public performances, rites are not carried through to the end.

102 top right
Cachoeira, a perfectly preserved colonial town in the State of Bahia celebrates the Nossa Senhora de Boa Morte Festival in August. The 200-year-old event commemorates the liberation of African women from slavery. Today it follows strict rituals, such as the request for donations, masses, processions, dinners, and samba de roda.

102 bottom right
Forty-five days after Easter, Pirénópolis, a colonial city 60 miles from Goiânia, capital of the State of Goiás, is the scene of the Divino Espírito Santo Festival. For three days it is the scene of tournaments, dances, and religious rites that culminate in the battle between Moors and Christians. The Moors are defeated and converted to Christianity.

102 top left
The congada *is a celebration typical of the northeast. It commemorates the coronation of a Congolese king during slavery.*

102 bottom left
In the Guerreiros, *a dance characteristic of the northeast, dancers dress in multicolored costumes and hats shaped like churches and decorated with mirrors and trinkets.*

Education also reflects an economic bias: More than 17 million people (more than 18% of the population over the age of 14) are illiterate, and the figure is expected to increase to 23 million by the year 2000.

The challenge of constructing a fairer Brazil has been taken up by Brazil's president, Fernando Henrique Cardoso, who included education among the priorities in his government's

manifesto. Has the time finally come when the gap between rich and poor, prosperous and destitute will be narrowed? Not many people think so.

This fatalistic outlook reflects one Brazilian characteristic; others include a sense of destiny, exaggerated optimism, delight in rhythm and color, and shameless nationalism. The nation's obsessions, samba, carnival, and football, translate these characteristics into practice and are vital parts of Brazil's culture. And Brazil's cultural practices often reflect its peoples' heritage: The samba was imported from Angola, while the carnival, introduced to Rio at the beginning of the colonial age, came from the Azores. Today, the samba schools parade in a Brazilian street specially designed for the purpose by Oscár Niemeyer. Called the "sambadrome," the street is almost

103 *The* Lavagem do Bonfim *is a traditional celebration held every January. After women dressed in white garments wash the steps of the Church of Nosso Senhor Bom Jesus do Bonfim, a great popular festival takes place. The sanctuary draws pilgrims from all over Brazil. Numerous miracles have occurred here, and the sacristy contains a remarkable collection of votives: plastic replicas of parts of the human body, crutches, plaster casts, and even bullets.*

104–105 Jangadas
*at anchor on a
Ceará beach. Fishing
is one of the main
activities in this
state, which includes
the Sertao, the
famous desert
immortalized by
Guimarães Rosa.*

104 top
*Fishermen on their
jangadas (rafts with
a small sail) return
to Canoa Quebrada.
This beach, in the
State of Ceará,
became a gathering
place for hippies in
the 1970s.*

105 top
Natal, the capital of the Rio Grande do Norte, is famous for its as yet uncontaminated beaches dotted with fishing villages and for the enormous sand dunes that constantly change shape with the wind.

2,000 feet long, with terraces on either side that can hold 6,000 spectators and is a monument to the Brazilian joie de vivre.

105 center
A street child (menino de rua) in São Paulo. Abandoned children are one of Brazil's greatest problems. They use drugs, steal to survive, and are persecuted by death squads that are often made up of off-duty policemen, who kill them without mercy.

105 bottom
The people of the northeast are a mixture of Indian, African, and Dutch heritage.

106 bottom left
The costumes of the filhas de santo, *the Candomblé priestesses, are modeled on those of the* Orixás, *the gods they impersonate. The girl in the picture portrays Oxúm, the goddess of the rivers, who corresponds to Nossa Senhora de Aparecida.*

106 top right
The cults of spiritism and Umbanda *are similar to Candomblé. But unlike Candomblé, in Umbanda rites communication with the spirits occurs through a medium, and the* filhas de santo *are not usually directly possessed by the spirit.*

106 bottom right
A filha de santo. *During ceremonies, the priestesses incarnate the saint invoked by the gathering and to whom they are devoted. Possessed by the god, the priestesses fall into a trance.*

106–107 *An initiation ceremony of a Candomblé priestess has a hierarchical structure, and rites are celebrated in specific places called* terreiros. *Candomblé initiation ceremonies are amply described by Jorge Amado, Brazil's most famous writer.*

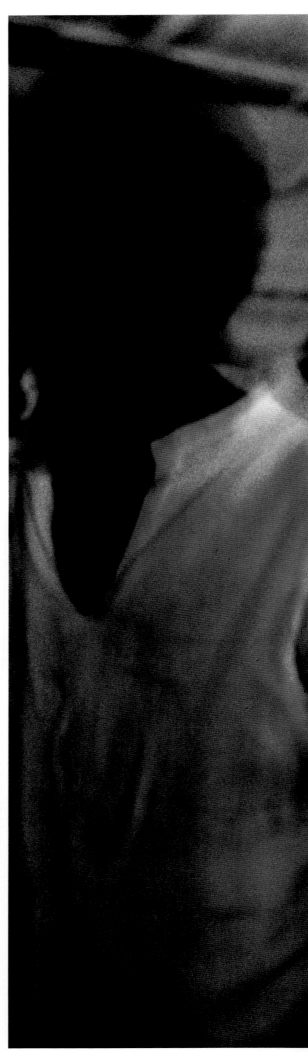

106 top left
A Bahian priestess of Iemanjá, the queen of the sea and fish. In the religious syncretism that mixes Catholic saints with African divinities (a ruse so slaves could continue to worship their own gods), the goddess of the sea corresponds to Nossa Senhora de Conceição and is portrayed as a siren with a woman's torso and a fish tail.

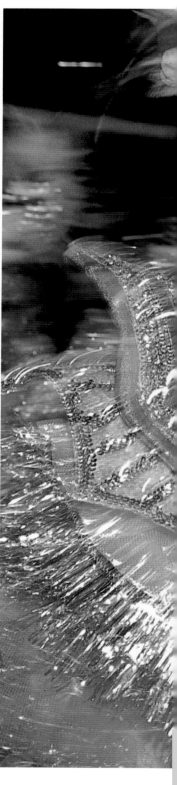

108–109 *Carnival is the most popular festival in Brazil. Imported from the Azores in the 17th century, the celebration reigns supreme in Rio de Janeiro. In 1934,* *during the government of Getúlio Vargas, the samba became the official dance of the Carnival and the symbol of this great festivity. Carnival is one of the few events* *that brings Brazilian society together: During this week, everyone meets for the "pular carnaval na rua," dancing the samba in the streets with no distinction of race or class.*

THE AMAZON, A LAND UNDER SIEGE

111 top
The great water lily (Vitória régia) has leaves that can grow 6 feet long and 12-inch flowers. The flower's petals open only at night. An edible flour is made from the plant's seeds.

111 bottom
When the rivers flood, pools form in the middle of the forest. Fish reproduce in the pools.

110–111 *Brazil has many other rivers, in addition to the Amazon, the great river that crosses Brazil to flow into the Atlantic at Belém. The largest tributaries of the Amazon include the Negro, Içá, Yapurá, and Trombetas rivers, to the left, and the Tapajós, Xingú, Javary, Jataí, Juruá, Tefé, and Madeira rivers, to the right, as well as the igarapés that often form after forest floods.*

110 top left
Because of high temperatures and heavy rains (94 inches per year), the Amazon soil is acidic and not very fertile. Trees survive in the humus produced by their own leaves.

110 top right
The Amazon fills more than half of Brazil (58.5%) and contains an incredible variety of plants and animals.

R aoni, a Kayapó chief, has a stately appearance and is wearing glasses, a pair of threadbare jeans, and a magnificent feathered headdress. His torso is decorated and a wooden disc is inserted in his bottom lip as a mark of rank. He walks into the office of the minister of the interior in Brasília carrying a TV camera. With him are a dozen members of the Kayapò tribe. The men sit down on the large black leather sofas, cross their legs, and wait, firmly holding onto their spears. They're here to talk to the minister about a delicate question: A TV crew from Rede Globo has entered their reserve and started filming without permission, and the Indians confiscated the camera. The Kayapó people will relinquish the camera, if the camera crew destroys the film. When the solemn act has been performed, the Indians leave as silently as they came. The man of government, in his impeccable gray suit, and the man of the forest, clad in little but his dignity, are worlds apart.

Few native South Americans survive in the rain forest. There were 3 million Indians in the Brazilian part of Amazonia before the Europeans arrived, but there are only 160,000 now, about 60% of the 270,000 Amerindians in Brazil. They include a few representatives from numerous tribes. Their diversity is reflected in their languages: 150 different languages, divided into 12 linguistic families, are spoken in Amazonia alone. Ninety-five thousand Indians live in the 216 areas officially registered and supervised by FUNAI (the National Indian Foundation), the government agency responsible for protecting them. These areas cover just over 136 million acres, 10% of Amazonia. The huge green area covers more than half the territory of Brazil; is divided among nine states (Amazonas, Pará, Acre, Maranhão, Mato Grosso, Tocantins, Amapá, Rondônia, and Roraima); is 2,000 miles long from east to west and 1,200 miles from north to south; and contains 30,000 classified species of plants, 15,000 species of animals, and only 10% of the country's human population.

Many Amazonian Indian tribes are Westernized, at least in terms of labor

112–113 *The encontro das aguas, the meeting of the waters, where the Negro River joins the Amazon. The rivers are different colors because they have different types of water. The water of the Negro River is acidic and without minerals. The Amazon is rich in sediment that gives it a whitish-yellow color.*

112 top left *The Iguazu Paranà, despite its width (about 8,000 feet), is scarcely navigable because of the numerous falls.*

112 top right *Most of the Amazon rivers are navigable, and the most common means of transportation is the gaiola, a boat with several decks that transports passengers and cargo.*

113 top *Belém, the capital of the State of Pará, is one of the most important cities in the Amazon basin and also one of the wettest in the world. The most famous place in town is the historic Ver-o-Peso market, which sells practically everything, from river fish (sometimes exceeding 6 feet in length) to medicinal herbs.*

113 bottom *Manaus is the capital of the State of Amazonas. Once famous for its rubber (it was one of the richest cities in the world at the end of the last century) today this city is known as a free trade zone and home of the Amazonas Theater.*

organization. Some Indians work as *seringeiros* (rubber tappers), others trade in wood, and others have set up well-equipped agricultural cooperatives. Few still live according to the ancient customs. The Amazon population also includes *caboclos* (people of mixed Amerindian and Caucasian heritage) and *cafusos* (people of Amerindian and black African descent). The native peoples have lived in the forest for centuries, exploiting its natural resources.

Amazonia is often wrongly believed to be no more than a large, unowned, uninhabited forest that anyone can occupy and exploit. That must have been the attitude of the latest wave of colonists, which was made up of foreign multinationals, large landowners, gold prospectors, and adventurers of all kinds. The delicate Amazonian ecosystem is continually threatened by new inhabitants. The gold rush, which began in the 16th century, has now reached intolerable levels. Sixteenth-century explorers were attracted by the legends of Manoa and its king, called El Dorado by the Spanish, who covered his naked body with gold dust every day. In 1540, Spanish explorer Francisco de Orellana crossed the entire Amazon basin in search of El Dorado. Accompanied by a handful of men, he reached his journey's end, but he found no trace of the gold or the king. He traveled through dangerous country and was the first to see what he described as "the tribe of women alone," the legendary Amazons after whom the forest is named. Manoa was probably discovered two centuries later by Francisco Raposo, a Portuguese explorer who described its impressive walls and great palaces. But the legendary city was never rediscovered. Perhaps swallowed up by vegetation, it is still dreamed of by present-day Orellanas.

Gold has been found in the area, however, and has attracted thousands of prospectors. The best-

known prospecting location (though there are hundreds like it) is the Serra Pelada, a mountain ridge where gold was discovered in the early 1980s. The mountain was riddled with holes within a few years. The tireless *garimpeiros* (gold prospectors), coarsened by fatigue and gold fever, climb up and down steep ladders carrying bags of earth to be cleaned and sieved. Today, the Sierra Pelada looks like Dante's Inferno, a mass of desperate men frenetically searching for a few nuggets of gold, like thousands of dirty, ragged ants living for an illusion.

In addition to having a devastating effect on the Indians, who were killed by disease or the prospectors' rifles, the arrival of the garimpeiros took an equally dramatic toll on the forest. The rivers contain large amounts of mercury, which is used to filter gold and is toxic to human beings; new towns have sprung up, upsetting the delicate balance of Amazonia; and landing strips and roads have been built. But the forest continues to reclaim its land as it fights to survive. Natural devastation is often accompanied by moral devastation. It is not unusual for Indian girls little more than 12 years old to be kidnapped and taken to the towns (if a huddle of tumbledown shacks can be described as a town) to satisfy the appetites of the rough garimpeiros.

114 top left, 114 right, 115 left, 115 right
All Indian tribes, the Kayapó in particular, devote great attention to the body. Tattoos, piercing, and shell necklaces are popular adornments. Indians also have exceptional knowledge of herbal medicine. Many Indian foods, including manioc, moqueca (a Bahian dish made with fish and palm oil), and paçoca (meat cooked with manioc), are commonly found in Brazilian cuisine.

114 bottom left
Raoni, the memorable chief of the Kayapó, wearing the traditional yellow headdress, sign of leadership, and a lip disk, is the most famous Indian chief. He traveled with British singer Sting to save the Amazon.

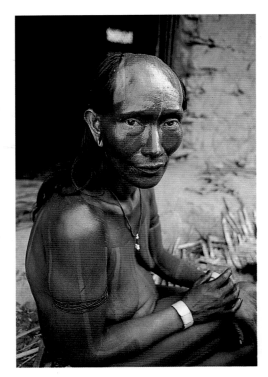

The Yanomami Indians inhale a hallucinogenic powder called yakoana through a bamboo shoot to combat disease and enter in contact with the hekurá, the eternal spirits of nature. The drug is extracted from the seeds of a plant in August and September, and only men are allowed to participate in the ceremony.

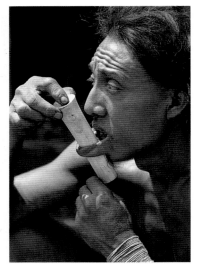

116 top left
The Barbudos Indians, a tribe recently discovered and apparently of Arara blood, are noted for their beards, an exception among the Indians who are normally smooth-skinned.

116 top right
The Poturú Indians, the tribe that lives on the banks of the Cupinapanema River in northern Amazon, pierce their lips to insert large objects, both for beauty and as a sign of leadership.

There is also a threat to the Earth's last source of oxygen. The government's campaign to populate the Amazonias region has brought in a throng of poverty-stricken settlers and rich landowners, all attracted by the rock-bottom prices of the land (6 acres cost as much as as two cows) and the hope of a better life. Hundreds of square miles of forest are burned each year to create pastures, in the belief that enough grass will grow to feed the herds. The effort is pointless, because Amazonias soil is not rich enouch to support grasslands. If the fertile part of the soil is destroyed, nothing else will grow. Fires leave the soil unprotected and open to erosion; they reduce fertility and cause floods and the formation of new islands that prevent underwater life and hamper navigation through the hundreds of rivers and streams that wind through the rain forest.

The list of invaders of the forest is constantly increasing. Some of the newer arrivals include aluminium factories that cause pollution, ironworks that use wood charcoal to fuel their furnaces and contribute to deforestation, and great hydroelectric plants that flood acres of forest without regard for the people or animals living in them.

But change is in the air. Since the involvement of Chico Mendes (the rubber tappers' leader who was killed by rancher Darli Albes), Sting, Raoni, the Rio Conference (a

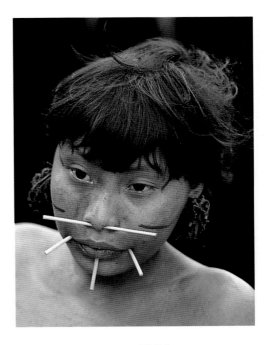

117 top
The maloca *or* aldeia *is the large hut in which the Indians live. Circular in form and open at the top, it houses numerous families.*

117 bottom
The Yanomami live in Roraima and part of the Venezuelan Amazon. They are known for the battles they fought against the large property owners and the garimpeiros, *who ten years ago invaded their territory with government consent (one of the sites for the mining of the precious metal was there).*

118 top left
Deforestation is one of the Amazon's greatest problems. Thanks to a media campaign by the Indians and international organizations, destruction of the great forest has been considerably reduced: the figure of 6 million acres razed in 1988 fell to over 2 million in 1991.

118 bottom left
Brazil's military dictatorship dreamed of a large roadway through the Amazon to link the Atlantic Ocean with the Pacific. Work began in the 1970s, but the vegetation grows so rapidly that it was impossible to open a permanent way through the forest.

118 top right
Seringueiros, *the rubber extractors, are fierce enemies of the* garimpeiros *and* fazenderos. *They have lived off the sap produced by the trubber trees for centuries and defend the forest from gold diggers and cattle breeders.*

118 bottom right
Garimpeiros *live a terrible life. They founded a shantytown in the forest and live without amenities. They also have regular clashes with the Indians, who perceive the miners as a threat to their land.*

major declaration of intent, but nothing more), and Marina Silva (a senator from Acre State and the latest champion of the rain forest), deforestation has declined. According to the official figures, it fell from 6 million acres in 1988 to 2 million in 1991—a promising trend.

Everyone should care about the life of the great forest, because the life of the Earth depends on Amazonia. Action must be taken before it's too late; the State of Rondônia has already lost 20% of its trees. The ideal solution would be to harvest the resources of the forest without destroying it. Apart from rubber and an immense amount of tropical fruit, the forest is also a huge pharmacy; 400 drugs have been developed from its plants so far.

A precedent for selective harvesting was set during the rubber boom at the turn of the century. Brazil sold 88% of the rubber exported in the world. The profits of the trade built Manaus. The symbol of the city's wealth is its opera house, built in 1896 at a cost of $10 million in today's dollars. The building's iron structure was assembled in Glasgow, the 66,000 colored bricks that decorate the dome were imported from France, and the frescoes were commissioned from Italian painter Domenico de Angelis. The port on the Negro River became one of the richest in the world. Manaus's power came to an end shortly before

119 Garimpeiros *have had a devastating impact on the forest. The only example necessary is the Serra Pelada, in Pará, where* thousands of gold prospectors have assailed a mountain and are gradually scraping it away as they search for just an ounce of gold.

120 top
The sloth (Bradypus
tridactylus) *is
jokingly called
"bicho pregiuça,"
lazy animal, by the
Brazilians because of
its exasperatingly
slow movements. This
apparently harmless
creature has a deadly
grip.*

120 bottom
The anta, *the
Portuguese name for
the tapir, lives all
over the Latin
American continent
and can grow to 3
feet in height and 6
feet in length and
weigh 400 pounds. It
feeds on a diet of
fruit and leaves and
lives near rivers.*

the World War I, when Asian plantations, controlled by the British, began selling their rubber at a lower price.

Those days are long past, swept away by relentless progress and a great, slowly flowing river. "The River Amazon," said author Mário de Andrade during a trip down the river in 1927, "is the final proof that monotony is one of the most magnificent elements of the sublime." How right he was. The landscape of the Amazon River and its 1,100 tributaries consists of mile after mile of trees. The river is navigable from Belém (in the State of Pará), where it flows into the Atlantic, to Iquitos in Peru, 2,300 miles away. The river is the natural highway of Amazonia. The explorer's dream, the source of life for thousands of species of plants and animals, including man, and a fount of legends, the Amazon stands guard over the forest.

A spark of life suddenly leaps out of the water and dives in again with a splash. It's a boto, a dolphin with a long nose that looks like a beak. In the forest's Umbanda, the Candomblé cultures, the animal's genitals are considered miraculous aids to love and fertility. We can only hope the great Amazon, and its many animal and plant inhabitants, will be left in peace in the coming years and that the human population will learn how to use the forest's resources carefully and wisely.

120–121 *The
numerous monkey
species that live in
the forest include
the nocturnal
monkey that is fond
of canebrakes and
feeds on the plant's
leaves.*

121 top
*Brazil has 450 species
of mammals, many of
which live in the
forest.*

122 *It is estimated that 1 square mile of Amazon forest contains more living vegetable and plant species than all* *Europe. More than 60,000 plant species have been classified in the Brazilian Amazon alone.*

123–126 *The Amazon is commonly known as "the lungs of the world." The forest actually produces precisely the amount of oxygen needed to keep its plants and living creatures alive. If* *anything, the Amazon is a reservoir of carbon dioxide from the fires that burn during deforestation. The carbon dioxide increases the greenhouse effect on the planet.*

127 *The Brazilian stretch of the Amazon River is fully navigable. The longest river in the world (4,247 miles), it averages 98 feet in depth, and in some parts, such as the Obidos Strait, it is 330 feet deep. The river's maximum width is 9 miles at the confluence with the Tapajós River, and during the rainy season the level of the river rises from 33 to 50 feet.*

128 top left
The tucanuçu *(Rhamphastus toco) of the toucan family lives in small colonies and nests in cavities in tree trunks. Toucan is also the name of an Indian tribe and a language spoken in the northwest Amazon.*

128 bottom left
Numerous animal species live in the Amazon, some not yet classified. The queen of the reptiles is the anaconda, sucuri *in Portuguese, a snake that grows to 33 feet in length. Grayish-green with symmetrical patches* and a yellow belly, it lives in the water and feeds on fish, birds, mammals, and crocodiles. The snake slowly squeezes its prey until all the animal's bones are broken and then the snake swallows it.

128 top right
Botos *are frequently spotted along the Amazon River They will appear suddenly and follow boats for long stretches. Their genitals (male and female) are dried and sold at the market as powerful love remedies.*

128 bottom right
There are 18 known species of piranha in Brazil. They range from 7 to 17 inches in size, and their incredibly sharp teeth make them a hazard for the inhabitants of the riverbanks. Extremely voracious, they are attracted by blood.

129 *The* onça pintada, *the jaguar, is one of the most feared mammals in the great forest. The jaguar can be found everywhere in Brazil except Rio Grande do Sul and the coastal states of the northeast.*

130–131 *Large, colored bracts enclose the small green flowers of the Heliconia* wagneriana, *one of the hundreds of plants growing in the Amazon forest.*

Mosquitoes and other small insects reproduce inside the plant's cavities, and birds (like this white-bearded hermit) come here to feed and consequently pollinate the heliconia.

130 top *Because of the humid microclimate, flowers are a characteristic of the great forest.*

131 top left *The jambeiro is a member of the myrtle family* (Eugenia malaccensis), *which originated in India. The plant has large, brightly colored, oblong leaves, conspicuous flowers with numerous stamens, and a tasty purplish-red fruit.*

131 bottom left *It is estimated that Brazil has 55,000 flowering plant species, most of which can be found in the Amazon.*

130 top right *The variety of plants in the Amazon is enormous. There are more than 400 known types of medicinal plants alone.*

130 center right and bottom right *Orchids flourish in Brazil. Many of the plants in the huge Amazon basin are also found in Africa, because the two continents were joined millions of years ago.*

INDEX

MUSEUM AND ART COLLECTIONS

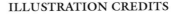

136 Arara *and parrots live in Brazi's immense* *pluvial Amazon basin and in Mata Atlântica.*